Hertfordshire Vol II

Edited by Lynsey Hawkins

YoungWriters
First published in Great Britain in 2004 by:
Young Writers
Remus House
Coltsfoot Drive
Peterborough
PE2 9JX
Telephone: 01733 890066
Website: www.youngwriters.co.uk

SB ISBN 1 84460 564 7

Foreword

Young Writers was established in 1991 and has been passionately devoted to the promotion of reading and writing in children and young adults ever since. The quest continues today. Young Writers remains as committed to engendering the fostering of burgeoning poetic and literary talent as ever.

This year's Young Writers competition has proven as vibrant and dynamic as ever and we are delighted to present a showcase of the best poetry from across the UK. Each poem has been carefully selected from a wealth of *Once Upon A Rhyme* entries before ultimately being published in this, our twelfth primary school poetry series.

Once again, we have been supremely impressed by the overall high quality of the entries we have received. The imagination, energy and creativity which has gone into each young writer's entry made choosing the best poems a challenging and often difficult but ultimately hugely rewarding task - the general high standard of the work submitted amply vindicating this opportunity to bring their poetry to a larger appreciative audience.

We sincerely hope you are pleased with our final selection and that you will enjoy *Once Upon A Rhyme Hertfordshire Vol II* for many years to come.

Contents

Wymondley JMI School

The Poems

My Imaginary Friends In My Life

When I was one, I had an imaginary dog,
It bit me!
When I was two, I had an imaginary cat,
It scratched me!
When I was three, I had an imaginary cheetah,
It was too fast for me!
When I was four, I had an imaginary rhino,
It charged at me!
When I was five I had an imaginary rabbit,
It hated me!
When I was six, I had an imaginary frog,
It leapt on me!
When I was seven, I had an imaginary tiger,
It nearly killed me!
When I was eight, I had an imaginary monkey,
I can't climb trees!
Now I am nine, I don't know what to have!
How about an elephant?
Yeah, but it is just mine!

Hannah Beech (9)
Arnett Hills JMI School

Riddle Of Books

Scrolls of knowledge
Writing of college
Yarn of Prince Charming
Tales quite alarming

Talk of a tree
Diary of thee
Literacy, art and ICT
And pages of numeracy.

Freddy Stokes (10)
Arnett Hills JMI School

EastEnders

Angie's Den got burnt down
Dennis went storming round the town
Vicky got trapped in the club
While Sharon was drinking in the pub
Kat and Alfie married in the end
And Andy went round the bend
The mini bus has a crash
And Zoe's leg got a bash
Little Mo ran away
After a tragic birthday
Den set up Phil
And Phil got taken down the *old bill*
Barry died when he fell on a rock
When Paul found him, he was in shock
EastEnders is the best! Better than all the rest!

Ashleigh Flood (10)
Arnett Hills JMI School

The Sunflower

The sunflower stands,
So tall and bright,
Its colours glowing,
In the light.

Yellow, green and white
Are the colours
Of the sunflower
Which stands so tall and bright.

The sunflower dances
Among the flowers and the leaves,
In someone's garden.
Is it yours?

Tori Elliott (10)
Arnett Hills JMI School

The Beast

In a deep, gloomy, pitch-black cave,
There lies a beast of many weapons,
It guards the gold of many colours,
For its life depends on it.

Many knights come to slay this beast,
But none live to tell the tale.
It has them all delightfully,
To crunch on their delicious bones.

I bet you think that it can only breathe fire,
But, ah, you are wrong,
It can also breathe ice
And shatter you into a million pieces.

So now I have told you this deadly tale,
I hope you don't go looking for this beast
Because if you do, you'll never live again,
For this beast can never die!

Karina Howlett (10)
Arnett Hills JMI School

K Howlett

Holidays Are Full Of . . .

H appiness
O n the beach
L aughter
I ndoor swimming pools
D ining out
A ll day spas
Y oung people having fun
S un and sand.

Lauren Bates (10)
Arnett Hills JMI School

Pop Stars

As a pop star you'll be seen,
Cruising around in a limousine.
All the hard work must be done,
But in the end is so much fun.

Then you get famous and be on television
And if you're a kid it would be a lot of confusion.
You still have homework and friends to think about
And still have to fight with Mum and refuse to eat sprouts.

I have dances to make and songs to write
And they have to do it day and night.
You promised friends to go shopping for shoes,
Uh-oh, oh no, what should I do?

I told my friend that I'm a big star now
And they calmed down after, I don't know how,
I took them on a trip to the health spa,
So now they're OK with me being a
Pop star!

Priyadharshini Shanthakumar (10)
Arnett Hills JMI School

It's A . . .

Towering inferno
Big banger
Fire spitter
People killer
House destroyer
Noisy roarer
Deadly pourer
Rocky island

It's a volcano.

Nick Mansi (9)
Arnett Hills JMI School

My Guinea Pigs

They are soft, small and come in all different shapes and sizes,
But my favourite guinea pigs are Snuffle and Truffle, my pets.
I think they talk but also sniffle and squeak.
They chirrup and chirp and sound like a bird,
A particular bird called a woodpigeon,
Coo! Coo!
But I love my boys just the same,
Coo! Coo! Coo!

Katherine Johnson (8)
Arnett Hills JMI School

A Cat Called Bell

On my 8th birthday I got a cat
All day long he sits on his mat
He has black and white fur
And really you should hear him purr

His eyes are a bright green
But sometimes he can be mean
He likes to catch mice
Which isn't very nice

He's got tiny little feet
But I think he's very sweet
This is a tale I like to tell
About my cat called Bell.

Nathan Rutter (10)
Arnett Hills JMI School

Funfair

'Mum, Mum, there it is
There's the funfair
Oh look, there's that game
That I won the stuffed bear'

What to go on first
I don't know what to pick
Maybe the mini roller coaster
Or the game with the wooden stick

'Mum, Mum, the swizzler!
Can I go on that?'
I went on that last year
With Sarah and Matt

I know what I'm going on
The big wheel looks like fun
Rocking backwards and forwards
And round and round I'm spun

'Mum, Mum, I'm hungry
Can I buy some candyfloss?'
'Darling, stop nagging
I'm starting to get cross'

The fair is so much fun
So many things to do
It's one of my favourite places
Is it the same for you?

Sian Tillott (8)
Arnett Hills JMI School

You And Me

You are my one,
My only one,
The one I shall cherish,
Forever and ever,
Wherever I go,
Whomever I meet,
I shall always think of you.

Rebecca Hales (11)
Arnett Hills JMI School

'Oink!' Said The Billy Goat

'Oink!' said the billy goat
Riding on a speedboat
'Woof!' said the cat
On the chair he sat
'Cluck!' said the pig
He went to a gig
'Moo!' said the duck
He had potluck
'Squeak!' said the tiger
She had a pint of lager
'Quack!' said the dog
Going to swim with a frog
'Coo!' said the donkey
Lost three legs and became a 'wonky'
The owl coughed and cleared his throat
As she began to bleat
'Bow wow!' said the cock
Swimming in the heat
'Baa!' said the hen
Writing with its pen
'Tu-whit tu-whoo!' said the farmer
He'd gone wrong too!

Tamsin Carter (8)
Bengeo Primary School

Miaow, Miaow, Kitty Rap!

'Miaow, miaow, kitty rap
Can you rap?'

Miaow, miaow, miaow, miaow, miaow
Miaow, miaow!

My cat go mad and swing their heads
Left and right!

They waggle their tails up and down!
I say, 'Can you rap kitties?'

Miaow, miaow, miaow, miaow, miaow
Miaow, miaow!

Their fluffy hair spikes up and up,
They swing their bottoms and eyes left and right!

'Can you rap kitties?'

Miaow, miaow, miaow, miaow, miaow
Miaow, miaow!

Rebecca Scott (9)
Bengeo Primary School

Oliver's Pets

In his bedroom Oliver kept . . .
Ten animals fighting,
Nine rhinos stamping,
Eight monsters eating,
Seven pterodactyls flapping,
Six parrots talking,
Four alligators snapping,
Three frogs leaping,
Two rabbits hopping
And one . . . guess what?
Me!

Oliver Hunt (9)
Bengeo Primary School

In My House There Are . . .

In my house there are . . .
Ten cats miaowing
Nine snakes slithering
Eight spiders crawling around
Seven shiny sharks relaxing in the bath
Six bunnies jumping around in the house
Five tigers roaring at the bunnies
Four turtles chugging along
Three puppies barking in the kitchen
Two butterflies fluttering in the living room
One dolphin splashing in the pond.

Toni Thompson (9)
Bengeo Primary School

Henry VIII

Henry VIII was big and fat,
Henry VIII broke a chair when he sat,
But when he was a prince, Henry was fit,
He also had style and wit,
Henry VIII had six wives,
Two divorced, one died,
Two beheaded, one survived,
But at the end, Henry wasted all,
Leaving his son with nothing at all!

Ilyaas Daar (9)
Bengeo Primary School

Hey, Teacher

Hey, teacher, come here, yo, yo, yo
We think you've got something that we don't know
So tell us now and we'll let you loose
Please tell us the secret cos we got the blues!
So you've told us the secret now
But what is that?
Tell us what that is inside that magic hat!
'Oh, it's just a little something that my father gave me,
But don't tell anyone cos otherwise you'll see
The end of your life is coming very soon,
So be off with you boy or else you're kicked out with a . . .
Bbboommm!'

Georgina Braggins (9)
Bengeo Primary School

Bosworth Rap

Richard III had the crown,
'Til Henry's army came to town.
They had a battle, arrows and shields
And brought along a sword to wield.
Henry Tudor made a deal,
But this time it was really real.
Then Richard III felt the sting,
Henry VIII, the new English *king!*

Hani Latif (9)
Bengeo Primary School

My Nan Can Groove

My nan can groove
She makes me smile
She keeps me grooving
For a little while
The groove is grooving
The move is moving
So let's get grooving
For my nan is moving
I like my nan because she's grooving
And plus she gets me in the mood for moving
The groove is grooving
The move is moving
So let's get grooving
For my nan is *moving!*

Kimberley Skidmore (9)
Bengeo Primary School

On My Face . . .

On my face are googly eyes,
that I use for spying on flies!

On my face are great big ears,
that I use for hearing fears!

On my face is a great big gob,
that I use for shouting, 'Frog!'

And on my face is a nose not clean,
because it's got things long and *green!*

Becky Turner (9)
Bengeo Primary School

Dolphin Rhythm

The rhythm is cool, the rhythm is fast,
The rhythm, the rhythm you just want it to last.

So come on everybody, let's speed, let's shout,
Let's knock on the door then speed once more.

Let's eat some chips, then speed some more,
Let's shout, let's yell, let's hit the floor.

So come on everybody, let's speed, let's shout,
Let's knock on the door, let's speed once more.

Yeah!

Hayleigh Dawson (9)
Bengeo Primary School

My Sister

She was cute my sister,
With bits of fluffy hair,
She was cute my sister,
Playing without a care.

She was funny my sister,
Falling over all the time,
She was funny my sister,
She'd never commit a crime.

She was naughty my sister,
Running away from my mum,
She was naughty my sister,
Always smacking my bum!

Catherine Durbin (8)
Bengeo Primary School

The Cat And The Dog's Walk

At moonlight and the gleaming light,
The dog takes his shimmering flight,
When the dog takes his moonlight walk,
He strolls and he sees a cat,
They have a talk,
Then finally they finish and they go on a stroll,
Daylight is here, they're still walking around,
Looking for something to eat on the ground,
Cat sees her owner, she has go to in,
The dog is lonely, no one to play with or have a walk, nothing,
The cat came out, they said they shall see each other again soon,
The dog was so pleased that he pounced with joy.

Sarah Phasey (9)
Bengeo Primary School

It's As Easy As . . .

It's as easy as getting a tree to smile
Or asking a planet to stop for a while.

It's as easy as getting a door to talk
Or asking your chicken to turn into pork.

It's as easy as getting a flower to sneeze
Or not getting stung by thousands of bees.

It's as easy as getting the moon to come out at midday
Or telling the water not to come to the bay.

Daniel Stephens (8)
Bengeo Primary School

A Knight In Shining Knickers

A knight in shining knickers cut his knee
He knew he shouldn't have done it
'But what the heck,' said he

A knight in shining knickers
Was at a football match
He was right behind the goalie
When he performed a great big catch

A knight in shining knickers had his head cut off
His mum was sad but said
'That will cure his cough!'

William Brant (8)
Bengeo Primary School

A Day In The Life Of Jodi, Our Dog

Jodi gets up,
Eats,
Runs round the garden,
Sleeps,
Gets up,
Chases a cat,
Eats,
Sleeps,
Goes for a walk,
Eats,
Sleeps!

James Lawson (9)
Bengeo Primary School

Spooks!

Every year in winter,
Inside the haunted castle,
Vampires, ghouls and ghosts
Hide in every nook and cranny,
Waiting for their chance to haunt the dirty, dusty basement,
Icy wind rattles the misty, murky windows,
On the moth-eaten sofa strange shadows
Appear out of nowhere,
The towering grandfather clock
Covered with silky spider webs!

Juliette Milic (8)
Bengeo Primary School

Skater Dude

The skater dude
Has some food
Comin' down the street
Havin' somethin' to eat
On his skateboard
Does a trick
Flips his board
Breaks a cord
Does a 180
He skates all day
He skates all night
He gives me a fright
When he shouts, *'Argh!'*

Oliver Knight (8)
Bengeo Primary School

Escape Of The Hamster!

Sniff, sniff
That smells good
Out of bed
Yawn and stretch
Look about
Ah peanuts
I must get them
Get the gnawing log
Aim at the cage door
Charge!
Smack! Crash! Bang! Wallop! Ow!
Aha, the door is open
I jump onto the door then the table
Fifteen centimetres jump down, can I do it?
I jump! Wahoo! I'm flying
Not for long, *owww!*
I made it
I run along the floor
I need to climb or jump one metre
Look, a ball of string
Nibble off one metre
I tie a slipknot
Aim at the peanuts
And throw, yes, on target
Now just to pull
Puff, pant, squeak, squeak,
Crash! Bang! Thud! The packet's down
I climb up the side of the packet
Jump in and . . . *eat!*

Andrew Mabbett (9)
Bengeo Primary School

The Sea

The sea is a place of wonder and exploring,
Going to the depths of eternity,
From sharks to squids and all types of fish,
It's really a great place to be,
You could swim for miles and not reach the end,
You can surf and water-ski till the moment you tie your boat at the quay,
The waves splash on the beach
And tempt you to go back in to unlock
The secrets of the wondrous sea.

Christian West (9)
Bengeo Primary School

Rapping Raptor

I'm a rapping raptor
I can rap all day

I'm a rapping raptor
I can rap, yeah!

I'm a rapping raptor
It is true

I'm a rapping raptor
Who makes a hullabaloo

I'm a rapping raptor
Who can do the tango

I'm a rapping raptor
I'm a dinosaur - yo!

Dan Gatfield (9)
Bengeo Primary School

Winter Falls

When the snow falls
It's like the twinkle from a star
It lands like a piece of cotton wool from a cloud

It covers the ground like a soft cushion
Snowmen get built so high, like people
But made out of snow

Children play in it and make footprints
Like they're drawing on a piece of paper

Then it melts like a disappearing act
It's not cold anymore
Winter has come and gone!

Emily Rudolph (9)
Bengeo Primary School

Hat-Trick Hero

There was a young footballer called Patrick,
Every game he played, he scored a hat-trick,
Suddenly his luck was over,
As he lost his lucky four-leaf clover,
As his mum set it alight with a matchstick.

Rebecca East (11)
Bournehall Primary School

There Once Was A Man From The Zoo

There once was a man from the zoo
Who went to Timbuktu
He thought it was funny
To buy two pots of honey
And stick himself to a shoe.

Ben Hammill (11)
Bournehall Primary School

A Ticking Clock

A ticking clock
It tells us the time every second, minute and hour
Tick-tock, tick
Like a soldier banging a drum
Like a brother or sister constantly thumping you on the back
It makes me feel sad and bored
An annoying beat that never stops
A ticking clock
It reminds me that life is precious
And short with the seconds ticking away.

Danielle Lipman (11)
Bournehall Primary School

Fall Down - Cinquain

Fall down,
Have a hurt knee.
Struggle to get back up.
Start to cry hopelessly, oh no,
Fall down!

Bradley Coleman (11)
Bournehall Primary School

My Dog Got Lost - Cinquain

My dog
Lost in a bog
And now he's gone for good
He was taken by a man in
A hood.

Tom Downes (11)
Bournehall Primary School

Jupiter, King Of The Gods

Jupiter, king of the gods,
A Roman legend,
Mighty, magnificent and mythical,
Like an unstoppable bolt of lightning,
Like a proud and fierce lion,
I feel worthless against his might,
Like a powerless slave,
Jupiter, king of the gods,
Reminds us of all that's powerful above the clouds.

David Goldsmith (11)
Bournehall Primary School

My Dog - Cinquain

My dog
Is a good dog,
He is always helpful,
He exercises all the time,
Like me.

Rinesh Patel (11)
Bournehall Primary School

The Man From Brazil

There once was a man from Brazil,
Who ate a dynamite pill,
His heart retired,
His bum backfired,
His head shot over the hill.

Ben Freedon & Ben Goode (11)
Bournehall Primary School

Sky

The gigantic sky,
Surrounds the planets,
Huge, massive, enormous,
Like a big jaw spitting
Out the weather,
It works like an untamable beast,
It makes me feel like an
Unknown lost baby ant,
Never to be found,
The gigantic sky,
Chooses the weather to match its mood.

Scott Turnley (11)
Bournehall Primary School

A Man Named Ted

There was a man named Ted,
Who blew up the garden shed.
His wife was mad,
He was sad
And now they are both dead.

Elizabeth Neale (11)
Bournehall Primary School

My Fish

My fish
Is dead, all she
Does is float upside down
So she will never swim again
Rip off!

Elliot Myrants-Wilson (11)
Bournehall Primary School

Seasons

In winter, snow falls,
Like great big halls,
Making days
With no netballs and footballs,
But the sun comes and calls!

The spring, the spring
Is a beautiful thing,
The flowers bloom,
In a lovely lagoon,
But we still have summer to come!

The summer is a great time
And in that time I start to mime,
But I still have time to drink my lime
And swim in the swimming pool,
But now the rain is coming again.

The leaves fall
On the brown muddy ground,
While I gather my money to a pound
And now that autumn
Is coming to an end,
Hello winter, we are back again!

Natalie Veiner (10)
Bournehall Primary School

A Star

A star
A boiling ball of gas
Hot, beautiful, bright
Like a sun burning in the sky
Like a fire burning in the wood
A star
Makes us feel good about the life we live.

D'anna Chambers (11)
Bournehall Primary School

Cinquains

The moon

The moon,
Floating in space,
Like a big piece of cheese,
Ready to explode anytime,
The moon.

A shoe

A shoe,
Old and tatty,
Never to be looked at,
Never to be taken note of,
Old shoes.

Daniel Johnson (11)
Bournehall Primary School

My Pets

Some that are fat,
I love my cat,
You have to brush their fur,
But be careful, some purr.

Some have sharp claws,
Some have little paws,
Some fight a lot,
But some do not.

Some play with a ball,
Some are very tall,
Some jump up,
Some jump down,
Some jump around and around and around.

Jessica Tadros (9)
Bournehall Primary School

The Scorching Sun

Thousands of times bigger than the Earth
Blistering, boiling, torrid
Warmer than the hottest fire
Brighter than the brightest torch ever
When the sun comes out it makes me feel happy
But as the day progresses
The sun gets to its full capacity of danger
The scorching sun
Reminds me how big our universe is.

Lorna Allett (10)
Bournehall Primary School

Summer

Sparkling summer
Gleams like Heaven
Bright, hot and beautiful
As hot as a fireball
Hotter than an oven
I feel cold like the Arctic
Shivering like an ice cube
Sparkling summer
Reminds me of life under the sun.

Danielle James (11)
Bournehall Primary School

Gravy

There was an old lady who worked in the navy
And she fell into a tub of boiling gravy
She thought it was fun
So she burnt her bum
And then she cried out, 'Someone save me!'

Mitchell Russell (11)
Bournehall Primary School

I Like The Way . . .

I like the way the birds sing,
I like the way the bells ring.

I like the way my dog goes woof!
I like the way a lamp goes poof.

I like the way a pencil writes,
I like the way a lion fights.

I like the way the stars shine,
I like the way you get a straight line.

I like the way I have all my friends,
I like the way the world never ends.

Laura Goldby (10)
Bournehall Primary School

My Cat - Cinquain

My cat
Went splat under
A car, I was upset
I went and got another one
Called . . . *Splat!*

Matthew Mason (11)
Bournehall Primary School

Netball! - Cinquain

Netball
Is a fun sport
You run around a lot
And try and catch the ball, caught it!
You win!

Charlotte Harrison (11)
Bournehall Primary School

Winter

There's a breeze in the air,
The sun's coming out,
The flowers are blooming,
But there's no need to shout!
The clouds are white
And the sky is clear,
Until somebody realised that
Spring is here!

Everyone's happy outside in the sun,
There's smiles on faces and all are having fun,
We're making the most of this beautiful day,
Until autumn has come and it's all gone away.

The leaves are falling off the trees,
There are no sounds of the buzzing bees,
The leaves are red, yellow and brown,
No more smiles, just some frowns!
Once again we've got nothing to do,
Can you guess it? I've given you a clue!

Winter is grey,
Nothing more I can say.
It snows and it rains,
On the windowpanes,
It's foggy and cold
And as I was told,
There's puddles and shivers
And even some quivers.

Natalie Parker (9)
Bournehall Primary School

Best Friends

Best friends,
Kind, fab, fun, cool,
Wanting to be around,
There for you whenever in need,
Best friends.

Sasha Badhan-Gill (11)
Bournehall Primary School

Abby, The Cat

There was a cat,
She was a pest,
She coughed up hairballs
That were a mess.

Her name was Abby,
She was a grey tabby
And she looked like
A bird's nest!

Ellen Hodgson (9)
Bournehall Primary School

The Door - Haiku

Hear these bells ringing
When someone rings the doorbell
Every day and night.

Charlotte Quarrell (10)
Bournehall Primary School

My Favourite Things

Salty and crunchy,
I love chips,
When I see them,
I lick my lips.

Sticky and chewy,
I love toffee,
When I eat it,
I dip it in my coffee.

Stripy and mysterious,
I love the white tiger,
When I get the chance to stroke it,
I'd probably run away, *'Argh!'*

Friendly and funny,
I really like my friends,
Whenever I am with them,
I know our friendship will never end.

Danielle Cox (10)
Bournehall Primary School

The Cat That Lived For A Day

There once was a cat called Ray
Who only lived for a day
He got run over
By a Land Rover
And was never heard of again!

Christopher Carter (9)
Bournehall Primary School

A Boy Named Bill

I knew a boy named Bill
He had some mental pills
He fibbed and lied
Then choked and died
And that was the end of Bill.

Will James (10)
Bournehall Primary School

My Favourite Thing

My favourite thing is a Care Bear,
I always care
For my bear
And always dare
Not to lose it.

I love them more,
They're not a bore,
I loved to cuddle them,
When I was ten.

They hated to get tobbled on,
Then I named one Ron,
When I got home it was gone,
Then I found Ron.

Kym Wyatt (10)
Bournehall Primary School

Don't Eat Paper

There once was a boy called Billy
He was very silly
He ate paper for breakfast
Sprinkled with dust
But soon he choked in front of Milly.

Elsie Ring (10)
Bournehall Primary School

The Nose Picker

There once was a girl called Rose
Who would continually pick her nose
She picked it so much
It developed a crust
And now she can't get into her nose!

Harriet Gumbs (10)
Bournehall Primary School

My Fish, Will

I once had a fish called Will
Who drunk until he was filled
Until one day he drank the whole tank
I had to put him on a bank
And that was when he died, poor old Will.

Chris Mellors (10)
Bournehall Primary School

Tom, The Bomb

There once was a boy called Tom,
Who loved to play with bombs,
He set one alight and got a fright
His mum sailed over the moon.

Jordan Lawrence (10)
Bournehall Primary School

Joee, Joee, Joee!

Joee, the koala lives in the zoo
Waiting for his dinner, chopped kangaroo
He has a friend terrapin who's six years old
He lives in the water, icy and cold!

Charlotte Liebling (8)
Bushey Manor Junior School

Dogs

Green dogs,
Mean dogs,
Never to be seen dogs.
Kind dogs,
Fat dogs,
Very dark and black dogs.
Clown dogs,
Frown dogs,
Mainly bright and brown dogs.
Red dogs,
Dead dogs,
Fascinated in sheds dogs.
Tall dogs,
Small dogs,
'We run into walls' dogs.
Kind dogs,
Blind dogs,
Simple to find dogs.
We all know about dogs,
They think they're the clever clogs,
So now I think we all know never to trust . . . *dogs!*

Oliver Counter (9)
Bushey Manor Junior School

Dolphins! Dolphins!

Dolphins, dolphins swimming in the sea
Swimming along very happily
Watch them play, dive and twirl
See them doing fancy swirls
Day and night they love to play
Come and join them another day.

Zacharesh Bingham Thaker (8)
Bushey Manor Junior School

Tear, The Pony

Tear, the pony
Munching the grass
Jumping a hedge
Then galloping around
Making a neighing sound!

Olivia Myrtle (8)
Bushey Manor Junior School

Sid The Snail

Sid the snail is very slow,
Off he goes with a ho, ho, ho!
Slithering on the ground,
Never to be found!
Sid the snail
Leaves a slimy trail!

Jerram Counter (7)
Bushey Manor Junior School

Tommy, The Tiger

Tommy, the tiger
Deep in the wood
Prowling through the jungle
Not pouncing
Being good
Now home for tea
Salmon would be nice
Fresh from the sea.

Kirstin Henley-Washford (8)
Bushey Manor Junior School

My Sweet Cats

My cats are sweet,
Almost good enough to eat,
They like to play outside
Where they run and hide,
They like to come to me because I am kind,
They like to watch the fish,
'Cause I know they would like them on their dish.
They like to sleep all day in a comfy bed of hay,
My cats can jump high,
My cats are very sweet.

Oron Sheldon (7)
Bushey Manor Junior School

Famous Wolf

I am a wolf
And I don't like you
I don't eat people
But you think I do
You try to kill me and my pack
But deer, hares and birds are my favourite snack
You call me big bad wolf
In the stories you tell
But I am brave and strong
And have a good sense of smell
I have good hearing
And sight to use when
I have to protect my cubs in my den.

Cameron Dall (8)
Bushey Manor Junior School

The Hungry Spider

Once upon a time, there was a spider
People were frightened of her
They called her creepy-crawlie
She built her web really neatly

Once upon a time, there was a hungry spider
She was looking for her dinner
She had big red eyes
She trapped some flies
That's no surprise!

Once upon a time, there was a tired spider
She had eaten her dinner
She was left with one quest
To find a place to rest
Her cobweb made a nice nest

Once upon a time, there was a sleepy spider
Most people do not understand her
They see her as an ogre
Their vision of her is so much wider
A fly or an ant they would prefer

Once upon a time, there was a hungry, tired, sleepy spider
In a corner hidden from any stranger
I think she is very bright
And she sends you her goodnight.

Zachary Zarzi (8)
Bushey Manor Junior School

Horse

H uge horses eat and eat.
O ver hurdles, horses jump.
R acing horses race like rockets.
S uper-fast, darting like a cheetah in the wild,
E xcited and trying to last another day.

Daisy Sheridan (11)
Danegrove Primary School

Keep Out Of My Room

Keep out of my room,
Otherwise you will face doom.
My room is strictly for me,
But the problem is I have no key.
Keep out of my room,
Otherwise my temper will go *boom!*

I've told you millions of times,
Unless you thought they were mimes.
There's nothing for you to see,
Unless you want a kick in the knee.

So keep out of my room!
(Or you will face doom!)

Joanna Evans (10)
Danegrove Primary School

The Soldier

This soldier's going to war
He wasn't worried till he saw bodies
And bodies covered in blood
Lying peacefully in the mud

There's the enemy in sight
Now he's getting ready to fight
'Charge!' the general screams
So they do in their teams

When they charge
With their swords so large
The first he kills
Blood spills
And so the war goes on.

John Nesbitt (10)
Danegrove Primary School

Football Stadium At Day

I see the fans cheering
As the players came onto the pitch
A Mexican wave is going round the stadium
The manager shouts
As the ref holds up a red card

I hear the National Anthem
As the hot dog sellers shout out adverts
The crowd scream and shout
As the whistle blows for the second half

I touch the sharp studs on David Beckham's boots
As I stand on the prickly grass
Holding up the World Cup won by England

I smell the cooking hot dogs
And the freshly-cut grass

I can almost taste the excitement in the air.

Hannah Veares & Elliot Leopold (11)
Danegrove Primary School

Fireworks

Banging loudly breaking the peace
Sparkling, hissing, crackling in the sky
Many eyes watching it shine in the sky
Many mouths oohing and aahing as it explodes
Taking its beautiful final form
Children sitting on parents' shoulders
And running around with sparklers clutched in their hands
Fireworks dying and the sparkle falling back to Earth.

Olivia Ferrar (11)
Danegrove Primary School

On The Beach

Feel the golden sand,
So soft and wet.
Feel the pebbles,
So smooth and wow, they come in so many different
colours and shapes.

Swim in the water,
So cool because it's not too hot or cold.

See the waves,
How big they are,
Carrying the rocks and putting them down.
Listen to the breeze,
Rushing past you and taking the sand with it.
See the sun,
Yellow and warm heating you up.

Listen to the seagulls,
How loud they are, giving you a headache.
Feel the seaweed,
Wow, so soft.
See the starfish,
So beautiful but yet so spiky.

See the fish swimming,
Look how beautiful they are.
Smell the crabs,
They smell like poo,
Now it's sunset and I'm tired,
So I'm going home to have some dinner.

Roshni Ghelani (11)
Danegrove Primary School

Tiger

Drinking water from the stream,
A harmless creature it may seem,
Until it starts to search for food,
You'll sense the danger and know you're doomed,
Hiding in the grass ready to leap,
Then diving on its prey in one big heap,
Its coat consisting of orange and black,
Mainly running down the side of its back,
Showing off his long sharp claws,
Chomping his meat between his white jaws,
So whenever the jungle is where you're at,
Try and avoid this dangerous cat.

Louis Ross (10)
Danegrove Primary School

By The Seaside

See the waves roaring at you,
as you're sitting on the golden sand,
at least there isn't dog's poo
and it's munch calmer than a rock band.

Smell the cool, salty sea,
As you swim with your mate,
It's a perfect place to be,
When you're on a romantic date.

Feel the cool air coming towards you,
Seashells so nice to listen to,
Seaweed always stuck to you like glue,
But down goes the sun,
Why? I don't have a clue.

Mathuta Nanthakumar (10)
Danegrove Primary School

Lee's Tea

I used to know a girl,
Her middle name was Lee,
She was the only one in my whole class
Who put nine sugars in her tea.
She didn't have a first name,
So we just called her Lee,
Some of us called her Cubey,
Cos she put nine cubes in her tea.

I didn't know how she drunk it,
All down in one big gulp
And the fact that she could whistle
As she emptied out her cup
And she didn't leave at the bottom,
One grain of a sugar lump.

Lee died when she was 12,
(Sugar levels far too high),
So when I drink my cups of tea
I see her smiling from the sky.

Heléna Rollason (11)
Danegrove Primary School

Beauty In A Mother

As our hands are joined,
The love shines pure,
From sadness to happiness
And maybe even joy,
Love and affection will always remain,
As a caring mother,
That is her name.

Megan Hughes (11)
Danegrove Primary School

The War Must End

The warrior on the next day is about to fight,
He can't sleep all night.

He dreams about him being dead,
No one knows what's going on in his head.

The next day he fights with all his power and might,
He waves his sword to attack,
And the enemy just fights back,
As he attacks he has fire-raging eyes,
He looks in surprise.

He sees a dead soldier and blood in the air,
But there isn't much to care.
The warrior carries on wondering what to do,
Wondering to kill who?
This warrior doesn't want to fight with all his power and might.
The warrior was taken away from his home
And now he's all alone.

When the war had finished,
The warrior's name was Clinninch,
Now the warrior's dead, someone chopped off his head.

One day a man was thinking at a pub drinking,
He asks his friend Khain, 'Why do we have war
For we get in so much pain?'
'I don't know,' answered Khain, 'but for sure
We should never have war again.'

Sebastien Flynn-Goze (11)
Danegrove Primary School

Alphabet Poem

A is for Andy who eats lots of candy
B is for Ben whose best friend is Sandy
C is for Camilla who is always sad
D is for Danny who is always bad
E is for Eden who eats eggs
F is for Frances who plays with pegs
G is for Gavin who likes to play hockey
H is for Harry who is very sloppy
I is for Ian who likes the police
J is for Jack who always wears a fleece
K is for Kate who likes her food
L is for Liam who is always in a mood
M is for Mick who likes to act
N is for Nicholas who has a cat
O is for Oscar who goes to the optician
P is for Peter who reads fiction
Q is for Quasi who is always up-to-date
R is for Rick who is always late
S is for Steph who likes Kelly
T is for Tom who is smelly
U is for Ursula who likes the zoo
V is for Vincent who likes Kelly too
W is for William who likes to ride a horse
X is for Xavier who likes tomato sauce
Y is for Yolanda who likes flowers
Z is for Zack who thinks he has powers.

Rui Marques (10) & Richard Seager (11)
Danegrove Primary School

An Alphabet Of Names . . .

A is for Andy who keeps lots of junk
B is for Bernard who dresses like a punk
C is for Cindy who eats lots of cake
D is for Derek who likes to bake
E is for Elle who fancies Mike
F is for Francis who loves to play on his bike
G is for Gary who plays the flute
H is for Helen who is very mute
I is for Isaac who likes to drink milk
J is for Janet whose hair is like silk
K is for Kenny who likes to date
L is for Lyndsey who's always late
M is for Mimam who likes peas
N is for Nancy who chases bees
O is for Oliver who likes cricket
P is for Peter who hits the wicket
Q is for Quaser who always gests lairy
R is for Ricardo who's always scary
S is for Stephanie who's a good sleeper
T is for Tara who is the football keeper
U is for Ursula who's got a cap
V is for Vixon who sits on a person's lap
W is for William who has long hair
X is for Xeres who has a toy bear
Y is for Yolanda who is a great friend
Z is for Zelda who drives me round the bend.

Natalie Kallend (10)
Danegrove Primary School

My Dog

My dog, Poppy
Is so soppy
She's just a ball of fluff
But sometimes gets a bit rough
When I walk her round the block
She ends up chewing my sock
When I take her home
She enjoys chewing her bone
Her breed is very rare
But she still acts like a bear
She sometimes plays on the green
But usually gets a bit keen
Her eyes are brown and saucer-like
I love my dog to bits.

Jordan Lewis (11)
Danegrove Primary School

Adventure

Down the river,
Up the stream,
Round the lake
And in the sea
Down and down, how far we go,
Where we go, we don't know.

So . . .

Up and up, how far we went,
Up out the sea,
Back round the lake,
So down the stream
And up the river,
So in house,
Safe and sound, just for now.

Reece Gardner (11)
Danegrove Primary School

Alphabet Poem (Colours)

A is for all the colours you've seen
B is for blue, bright in the sky
C is for cheerful bright green
D is for dark red in the middle of a pie
E is for each and every kind of pink
F is for funky, funky maroon
G is for the great colour of the bathroom sink
H is for Henry's silver spoon
I is for indigo, sharp in the night
J is for jade, the colour of my wall
K is for khaki, the suit the army uses to fight
L is for lilac, the colour of the mall
M is for mauve, bright and shiny
N is for the nice colour of jeans
O is for olive, black, nice and shiny
P is for purple, the colour of kidney beans
Q is for the Queen's aqua throne
R is for the red rubies on my ring
S is for Sue's white ball she throws
T is for tea, brown, brown things
U is for my umbrella, stripy yellow
V is for violet, the colour of my shoes
W is for clear water, calm and mellow
X is for excellent gold earrings that come in twos
Y is for a banana yellow
Z is for zebra, black and white.

Sasha Thomas & Lucy Nevile (11)
Danegrove Primary School

Shark

S harks swim in the sea
H unting people that come to their territory
A shark is very fast
R escue boats come last
K ites are in the shape of a shark.

Jake Field & Joe Farley (11)
Danegrove Primary School

A Man From China

There once was a man from China
Who was a very good climber
He slipped on a rock
And broke his clock
And now he's got a timer.

Mark Dunstain Mwaungulu (11)
Danegrove Primary School

Girls

Girls are really nice,
But they don't like mice.

Some can be sporty
And others can be naughty.

They laugh at jokes,
But they don't like their folks.

Some like boys
And others like toys.

Vicki Thomas (11)
Danegrove Primary School

Nile Crocodile

Snapping, menacing jaws
With huge slashing claws

For you must know if on the Nile
Never smile at a crocodile

He would have you for his lunch
He'd eat you up in one big munch

And then he'd say, 'Who's smiling now?'
As he raised a green eyebrow.

Katie Beer (11)
Danegrove Primary School

Women!

Women always painting their nails
Not enough time to be with us males

Women always talk on the phone
And always forget to pay the loan

Shopping this, shopping that
I could hit them with a bat

Women always buying shoes
They think they have no money to lose

Women, what can you do with them?

Roey Livne (10)
Danegrove Primary School

Rabbit

R unning round the garden looking for bright green lettuce
A n ear pokes up, aware of different sounds,
B ouncing up and down when he sees his owner with his food,
B umping his foot on the floor when he is angry,
I nterested in whatever is around him,
T eeth always biting bright orange carrots.

Alex Kalogirou (11)
Danegrove Primary School

Adults

A lways
D ooming
U tterly
L oud
T error
S oldiers.

Maria Gerasimova (10)
Danegrove Primary School

Is Noah True?

What is Noah's ark?
A massive boat made out of bark.

The animals walking two by two,
But whoever said their story was true?

How could that boat take such weight
With the hippos and elephants lined up straight?

Travelling in the ocean wide,
It must have been a bumpy ride.

How were they supposed to dock
With their massive animal stock?

Is this how the story goes?
Most likely not, but nobody knows!

Nicky Mann (10)
Danegrove Primary School

Kat With A Bat

There was a girl named Kat
Who found a baseball bat
She swung it around
Then hit the ground
And one of her toes went *splat!*

There was a girl named Kat
And one of her toes went splat
She cried out in pain
Again and again
And then tripped over her cat!

Ben Summers (11)
Danegrove Primary School

My Family

They're a poem written by the hands of God,
They're as comfy as a room full of feathers,
They're as innocent and as kind as the dove that told Noah
the flood ended,
When they smile the whole world shines,
When they're upset the whole world is boring and cold,
They listen to you like Santa does at Christmas,
When they're happy they look like a midsummer sunset
And a swan swimming in the twilight,
They're as beautiful as a rainbow,
They share like husband and wife,
My family is the best ever!

Maria Anna Pachomiou (11)
Danegrove Primary School

A Girl's Favourite Things

Here is our poem on our favourite things
It includes stuff like diamonds and rings

We both like animals and our pets
Also we love our jewellery sets

Next along our favourite things line
Is our music we play all the time

Shoes are brilliant, they are the best
But slouch shoes are better than the rest

Our favourite shops are QS and many more
But you can't shop for too long or your legs will get sore

Diamonds and rings are a high price
But I have to admit they are very nice

There's many more on our list
But we'll be here for ages, we insist!

Melanie Steele (11) & Lucy Neville (10)
Danegrove Primary School

Our Favourite Things

A is for attention in big proportions
B is for bags and bangles that match
C is for clothes, so many in a shop
D is for diamonds and diamante that match
E is for end of school, we hope it comes soon
F is for friends forever we will be
G is for groovy girl's night out
H is for holidays in the hot, hot sun
I is for ice cream in all different flavours
J is for Ja Rule rapping his songs
K is for koalas, so cute and cuddly
L is for lipgloss, so clear and shiny
M is for make-up, so many different types
N is for nails with a cool French manicure
O is for O channel, we love the music
R is for resting while listening to music
S is for shoes with a thin high heel
T is for Top Of The Pops on TV
U is for umbrella, so we don't get wet
V is for very, very big shopping spree
X is for all our excellent CDs
Y is for 'Yeah', Usher's new single
Z is for zap! Make all these come true
Now our poem is finished too.

Laura Kline (10) & Beth Wilson (11)
Danegrove Primary School

Karate

K icking in the air
A ttacking your enemy
R eally enjoy it
A fun hobby
T he teacher is called Sensei
E xcellent if you reach your black belt.

Hasibe Yilmaz (10)
Danegrove Primary School

Alphabet Poem Of The Simpsons

A is for Apu the shopkeeper
B is for Bart, Lisa's brother
C is for Chief Wigum, the police officer
D is for Dr Hibbert, doctor of the town
E is for Edna, Bart's teacher
F is for Flanders, the Simpson's neighbours
G is for Grampa Simpson
H is for Homer, Bart's dad
I is for Itchy, the mouse in Itchy & Scratchy
J is for janitor Willie, the school's janitor
K is for Krusty the Clown
L is for Lisa, who loves her sax
M is for Moe Szyslak, the guy in the pub
N is for Nelson, the school bully
O is for Otto, the bus driver that takes Lisa and Bart to school
P is for Principal Skinner
Q is for Mayor Quimby
R is for Rod Flanders, son of Ned Flanders
S is for Snowball II, the cat
T is for Tod Flanders, brother of Rod
U is for United States - home to The Simpsons
V is for Van Housten, Milhouse the nerd
W is for Waylon Smithers
X is for all these excellent characters
Y is for you must watch The Simpsons sometime
Z is for zillions of laughs which you have when you watch the shows.

George Grogan (10)
Danegrove Primary School

Red

Red is the pain of blood oozing out
Red is the strawberry sauce on my 99
Red is the smell of a tulip
Red is the sound of the drops of blood, drip, drip, drip.

Akira Roberts (11)
Danegrove Primary School

The Beach

The romantic sunset starts setting down,
While the clashing waves calm down,
As the colourful fishes swim up and down,
As the seagulls and birds soar down.

Feel the cold breeze go past you,
Feel the golden, soft, squishy sand,
Feel the slippery, spiky starfish,
Feel the beautiful carved shells.

Listen to the wiggly seaweed,
Smell the crusty, smelly crab,
Smell the cool, salty water,
Smell the food from the café.

Listen to the seashell,
Listen to the calm waves,
Listen to the angry seagulls squawking,
Listen to the cool breeze.

Let's go home and have some dinner,
Let's go home and play with my sister,
Let's go home and go to sleep.

Come back tomorrow to play with the sea.

Vaishnavi Gnanakumaran (11)
Danegrove Primary School

Popeye

Popeye the sailor man,
He lives in a garbage can,
He turned on the light
And started to fight,
He's Popeye the sailor man.

Jesse Ross (10)
Danegrove Primary School

My Alphabet Poem

A is for apricot, all orange and soft,
B is for ball like a scrunched-up cloth.
C is for cupboard to hang all your clothes,
D is for doorknobs that don't have toes.
E is for evidence, to look for a clue,
F is for fantastic, who I think is you!
G is for gorilla, quite big but not nice,
H is for hockey, a game on ice.
I is for igloo, made of ice which is cold,
J is for jeans, which never grow mould.
K is for kangaroo, which can jump quite high,
L is for lolly, which doesn't give you exercise.
M is for Miss Danker, whose job is to teach,
N is for nappies, which cost fifty pence each.
O is for orange, as orange as can be,
P is for pencil, that's sharper than me.
Q is for the Queen who is rather posh,
R is for rabbit who I've never washed.
S is for singing that most people do,
T is for toilet, which is also called loo.
U is for umbrella, that stops you getting wet,
V is for victory, which I don't really get.
W is for work that we do at school,
X is for xylophone which isn't that cool,
Y is for yellow, a colour I like,
Z is for zebra crossing, where I ride across on my bike.

Clarissa Nicolaou (10)
Danegrove Primary School

Cat

Cat
Was slyer
Than fox
Prowling through the gardens
Eyes like bush babies
Hidden in the greenery
Senses twitching
Ears extremely eager
Listening through the night

Cat
Was mystery
That struck at any time
For she raced into danger
Waited for revenge
That was ready for her
And was armed.

Amy Gray (11)
Green Lanes Primary School

Candles

The presence of a flickering candle,
Chases shadows out of existence,
The soft, wispy tendrils of smoke,
Fills your nose and mouth, banishing fear,
A haze of light blinds your eyes,
Hypnotising you out of your worries,
Gloom scurries away, petrified of its peaceful glow,
The calming smell of silky smoke,
Urges you to let go of troubles and problems,
The light can sweep like a wave over the world,
Penetrating into the heart of evil and destroying it,
All the candles in the world are lit,
In churches, in homes, in you,
They burn brightly every Christmas Day,
When we celebrate the greatest light of all.

Hannah Maxwell (11)
Green Lanes Primary School

Cat

Cat
Slyer
Than stealth
Climbs up a tree
Ears like pointed witches' hats
Rests on a tree top
Fur as golden as the sun
Teeth ready to bite
And gnaw

Cat
Is a killer
That rips up its prey
Eats it in shreds
Looks up and pounces
With strong, silent movement
It picks up its speed and runs.

Jack Chilton (10)
Green Lanes Primary School

A Week

Monday swimming water
Like a river running
Down my back collecting in a pool

Tuesday music
Violins screeching, clarinets booming
Music dominates the air

Wednesday dancing
Swooping in and out
Of arched arms stretched out

Thursday choir
Voices ringing out
As clear as bells

Friday nothing
Bags scooped from the cloakroom
Then home.

Kirsty Dyce (10)
Green Lanes Primary School

Candles

Can you hear
The flickering?
Can you see
The flame?
Every time you
Light a candle
Jesus Christ is risen again

Can you feel
The peace?
Can you smell
The smoke?
Every time you
Watch a flame
Jesus Christ is risen again

Can you see
The beauty?
Can you feel
The safety?
Every time you
Approach a candle
It melts away
All your fear.

Phoebe Burgess (11)
Green Lanes Primary School

Cat

Cat
Is more devious
Then the slyest predator
Prowling through the night
Eyes like full moon
Silent on a fence
Tail up in the air
Hunting through his habitat
Ready to plunge and plunder
His prey

Cat
Is defender of the night
Creature of its grounds
Crouched on the dewy grass
He crept through the night
Mindful of fear

Cat crept - miaow, miaow.

Charlotte Jonah (10)
Green Lanes Primary School

Black

The mind of a forgotten child
The heart of evil
A gloomy mountain top
The screams of fear

The cold silence of death
The roar of thunder
The cries of a baby
The soul of darkness

The sadness of tears
The longing of space
And one colour not to mess with
Or you'll be sorry.

Katie Norfolk (11)
Ladbrooke JMI School

White Wolf

He wanders the world alone, a silent, solitary killer
A shadow hunter, deadly in all his supremity
His mournful howl pierces the forest from the icy heart
And all through the needle point mountains
He treads the ledges, not lifting a twig, slipping swiftly
His sleek, streamlined body sails over the ice
Rips through the night like a bullet in a frosty snow dome
Encrusted in frost, annihilating everything in its way

His growl tears through the darkness, enchanting the forest
In a spell of terror, he reigns over the north, king of the woods
His claws shatter the earth he walks upon as if it were
Bowing to the majestic white wolf leaving a mark of his arrival
His teeth as sharp as knives, rock hard like stone strike fear
Into the heart of all beings, his fur is soft and white
Like the snow around him, his tail swishing gracefully to and fro,
Tingling with frozen dewdrops, his gleaming eyes glow, golden
In the night, flashing like diamonds
Prince of the mountains, the white wolf.

Cristina Trujillo (11)
Ladbrooke JMI School

The Wolf

The wolf that lurks in the snow
Awaiting a chase for food
To come along expecting nothing
A hare bounds along, *bang*, there goes the chase
The wolf is victorious, the chase is done
The hare has lost, the wolf has won
The hungry wolf eats his win of food
Then it pounds off into the distance
He travels a mountain and howls to the golden moon
At midnight the wolf runs down as fast as a cheetah
As he thinks he is a cheetah pounding along
As he leaves pawprints in the soft soothing snow.

Rhianne Halsey (11)
Ladbrooke JMI School

Gorilla

The gorilla
Hunts in the jungle

Waiting for his prey
In the thick bushy leaves of the trees

Standing on its big knuckles
Breathing heavily

His shadow stretching out
Into the distance

He sees his prey
Slowly walking towards him

The prey did not see the gorilla
Waiting quietly

The gorilla pounced on his prey
Crushing all its bones in its body.

Edward Woods (11)
Ladbrooke JMI School

Alien

There's an alien in my bedroom Mum,
I'll tell you what it's like,
Its head is like a big balloon,
Its body like a stick,
Its claws are like swords
And it has teeth like daggers,
Its tail is like a needle,
Its feet are like sausages.

I know you don't believe me Mum,
But hurry up, it's getting closer,
It's . . . *aarrgghh!*

It's my brother!

Joseph Lang (11)
Ladbrooke JMI School

Red

Red,
Red is as angry as a swarm of bees,
The heat of boiling bubbling lava,
The fear of a soldier before battle,
A flame flickering.

Red,
Red is the aggression of bees stinging,
The rumble of an erupting volcano,
The violence of a terrible war,
A flame flickering.

Red,
Red is as deep red as dripping blood,
The depression of a burning house,
The fear of entrapment,
A flame flickering.

Red,
Red is the sadness of death,
The destruction of an explosion,
The scorch of a lightning bolt,
A flame flickering.

Craig Newton (11)
Ladbrooke JMI School

Water

Water is free,
Water is the life to keep us cool,
Water helps us think like the king of the sea,
Water is home to the merpeople,
On top of water is where the white horses hit the land and disappear,
Water eats whales,
In the water is the circle of life,
Water is a spirit,
Water is an item.

Mikey Brown (10)
Ladbrooke JMI School

The Ocean

Dark and mysterious,
The enchanting ocean sleeps
Like a rare jewel in the evening,
Salty tears the ocean weeps.

Dolphins, sharks and fish,
Live their lives in the bottomless ocean . . .
And when at night its waters gleam,
Its ripples release their aromatic potion.

When the lands and docks seem to run away,
The cold, chilly winds whip your face,
When the sunset is a sheet of silk,
Freedom welcomes you with a warm embrace.

Sparkling like precious diamonds,
Shimmering in the morning sun
And for that first time you see the ocean,
Your life has just begun.

Alexia Karageorghis (10)
Ladbrooke JMI School

Hurricane

The hurricane goes swaying
And dancing down the roads of Potters Bar.
Destructive, dirty, howling,
Scaring everyone off.
How do you think it feels,
Coughing, sneezing and spinning all day?
With not a care in the world,
It is destructive as a nuclear bomb,
As powerful as a crane,
It is furious and a spinning tube of wind.

Luke Wilkinson (11)
Ladbrooke JMI School

Alien Invader

Lurking among the dusty old boxes,
In the cupboard under the stairs,
With eyes as bright as foxes',
The daring creature prepares
For a mission as exciting as a movie,
The return to his spaceship, so dazzling and groovy.

The little green alien with a cheeky smile,
Had spikes on top of his head in a pile.
His umpteen feet like seals' flippers
And for his hands he had crab-like nippers.
He wobbled like a jelly
And shoved the door open with his belly.

Like a whippet he ran,
Almost knocking over Gran,
He flew out of the door
And could not believe what he saw.
Like a jewel in the crown,
His spaceship coming down.

Lucy Bevan (11)
Ladbrooke JMI School

An Alien Comes To Stay

The bright lights appeared in the sky,
Flashing and twinkling like a demon's eye.
The huge craft landed in front of my house,
I scampered to see it as quiet as a mouse.
Where did it come from, Neptune or Mars?
It sparkled and shone as bright as the stars.
I looked around the side and what did I see?
A short, stubby alien as green as a pea.
As it walked towards me I screamed with fright,
It opened its mouth, full of teeth as black as the night.
It jumped straight at me, I thought it was the end,
Until it said, 'I come in peace, will you be my friend?'

Jess Pott (11)
Ladbrooke JMI School

News Flash

News flash:
A paper plane
Dropped a purple soot bomb
On Tony Blair's head at his house
Not good

Sports news
A 10-0 win
Over Tottenham now
By Arsenal who thrashed them dead
Losers

Headline
The Queen's puppy
Pooed badly in palace
Queen was not a happy chappy
Mad Queen

The Queen
Went into street
An extra big beans tin
Squashed into flooded manhole
She stank

New news
An elephant
Escaped from Windsor Zoo
It body-slammed every school
Hooray!

Christopher Heron (11)
Ladbrooke JMI School

Nice Cars

It's nice
Can zoom well fast
And shoot past anything
Jaguar XJ3220
For me

Wing doors
Fancy and new
It's a car just for you
It's Mercedes Maclaren
Lovely

Cool car
Flies on the road
Can get past anything
Lamborghini Murchalago
Well nice.

Anthony Antoniou (11)
Ladbrooke JMI School

Candle

A flick of a match
And I am alight
Glowing all the time
Making a waxy river

I cough and choke
Fighting to stay alive
From the harsh wind
Coming from the mouth

As I get smaller and smaller
I know my life is running out
I will carry on fighting
But in the end I will flicker and die.

Jenna Doran-Twyford (11)
Ladbrooke JMI School

The Slithering Silky Snake

The slithering silky snake
Is a crafty fox.

It's as smooth as a feather
And is a killing carnivore.

It's as deadly as a dragon
And is a bendy pipe cleaner.

It has ferocious fangs
And is a raging reptile.

It is a long piece of rope
And is as bright as the sun.

It has penetrating poison,
Which forces you to death.

It is as camouflaged as a chameleon
And is a scaly crocodile.

David Bidmead (11)
Ladbrooke JMI School

Football

Football
Kicking a ball
About and scoring goals
Every day I play football with
My mates

Goalies
Taking goal kicks
Saving the ball from shots
Saving penalties and free kicks
He scores.

Daniel Philpot (11)
Ladbrooke JMI School

The Colour Red

Red is as deep and lonely as depression,
Red is like a frightening bloodthirsty war,
Red is alerting and quick like danger,
It carries burdens of the Devil,
Red is as hot as exploding lava,
But it can be as sad as the last red rose being laid on a grave,
Red has the anger of being led into betrayal,
It also has the sadness of a widow,
Red is a quick murder,
Red is as scary as a November night,
Red is like being plunged by a sword and the dark of
death approaches,
Red is the colour of red rosy lips like a kiss of death,
Red is like one last lie,
Red is as raged as a fire,
Red is like the last petal of a flower falling showing all hope is lost.

Jordan Rutnam (11)
Ladbrooke JMI School

Alien

There's an alien in my bedroom, Mum,
I'll tell you what it is like,
Its head is like a baked bean,
Its body is as thin as a matchstick,
Its claws are as sharp as pins,
Its teeth are as sharp as needles,
Its eyes are like cricket balls,
Its hands are like the paws of a tiger,
Its ears are as big as the FA Cup.

I know you think I'm lying, Mum,
Hurry up it's getting nearer,
It's getting closer
It's . . . *argh!*

Josh Smith (11)
Ladbrooke JMI School

Christmas Day

Look up . . .
The snow floats down
Around are white wonders
In the house a family gathering . . .
Happily

Christmas time . . .
A family tradition
Of giving and taking presents
To celebrate Jesus' birthday . . .
Happy times

Out front . . .
The frosted streets
Sparkle especially like a
Street of diamonds shining as bright as . . .
Sunlight

Playing . . .
Children play out
In the snow having fun
Laughing all the way, sledging down hills . . .
Cheerfully.

Jack Webb (10)
Ladbrooke JMI School

The Whale

The whale is big, as big as a ship.
The whale is strong, as strong as iron.
The whale is loud, as loud as a jet.
Once it got caught in a giant fishing net.
The whale is mighty, as mighty as God,
It's a miracle the whale can fit into the sea.

Sophie McKee (9)
Ladbrooke JMI School

The Moon And The Sun

During the day the sun sings
Dancing amongst the clouds
Laughing to the sky
And telling jokes to its friends
Singing with glee
Watching over me

Floating in the sky
Watching over the people
Like a king to his kingdom
When all of a sudden the lights turn out
The sun is covered by a sheet
And for a moment the sun and the moon meet

The sun is replaced by the moon
A black blanket full of stars fills the sky
The moon whistles to the stars
It howls like a wolf
A mirror ball in the sky
Shooting stars zoom by

The moon whispers to itself
Telling itself wonderful stories
It sprinkles glitter on the stars
To make them shine longer
Spreading its happiness throughout the night
Reflecting the sun's powerful light

The process starts again
Repeating itself to make night and day
Smiling throughout the year
Keeping everybody happy
Spreading its joy through everyone . . .

That's the cycle of the moon and the sun.

Hannah Norfolk (11)
Ladbrooke JMI School

Hurricane

I am the hurricane
My winds are as hard as rocks
And when I am angry
I crush people with my wind

I am always frowning
People do terrible things
And when they do I scream and shout
But they don't hear me
I make big winds that throw them into walls
Then they hear me

Nobody can see me
I am invisible
But I do have feelings
Which people hurt
So I make disaster
Then they hear me.

James Bowman (11)
Ladbrooke JMI School

Turquoise`

As relaxing as a cool breeze
As mystical as a magician
As gentle as a mother's touch
A peaceful sound
A deserted child
A death-beckoning silence
A glinting aquamarine
Hidden in the night
A rewarding blue
And a wavy sea
That brings a chill to me.

Nathan Lister (11)
Ladbrooke JMI School

The Sun

A round ball of fire
Which stands up high in the sky
And jiggles about all day
Trying to push past the clouds
To release its wonderful rays of light

Once it comes out
The sun breathes upon people
Living on Earth
And runs round the world 24/7

At the end of the day
The sun is still out
But sleeps for the night
While the moon comes out
And sets alight.

Patrick Metselaar (11)
Ladbrooke JMI School

Large Mammal

It is grey
It can crush you
It can spray water
It is quite a dangerous animal
It has got three nails on every foot
It can swim only on the surface
It is big and fat
It is sometimes white
Its tusks are long and yellowy
A catalogue
To make an elephant.

Joseph Field (10)
Ladbrooke JMI School

Midnight

It's the middle of the night and I'm hungry,
I got out of bed and tiptoed down the stairs,
What would I like to eat, maybe some pears?
When I'd fixed myself a snack,
Out of a biscuit pack.

I turned my back,
When I turned around,
I saw a mouse on the ground,
My snack was gone,
I hadn't been round for long.

I knew the culprit was the mouse,
I wondered how he had got in the house.
I ran upstairs and almost tripped
Over a bedroom chair,
I jumped into bed
And almost bumped my head.
Now I didn't want a midnight feast ever again.

Bethany Brett (9)
Ladbrooke JMI School

End Of Term

No more homework, hip hip hooray,
No more teachers talking all day.
No more sun and Earth and moon,
We'll open up our Easter eggs soon.
No more people shouting all day,
Cos we'll be on holiday.
No more lovely ICT,
Cos we'll be right by the sea.
No more science, that is fun,
Cos we've learnt about the sun.

Edward Hull (8)
Ladbrooke JMI School

Worm

Wriggly worm *run!*
Wiggly wiggerly worm *run!*
For I am coming

Juicy worm *run!*
Juicy worm *run!*
For I am coming

You are the prey
I am the predator

Wriggly worm *run!*
Wriggly worm *run!*

Too late *munch!*
Munch, munch!
Munch!

Christian Archer (9)
Ladbrooke JMI School

Celebrities

Starring in a movie,
Singing on Top Of The Pops,
Dancing groovy,
Wearing crop tops.

On TV all the time,
Getting lots of money,
In America they call you 'Honey',
I know, it sounds funny.

People doing your hair,
People choosing your clothes,
If you're famous, people stare,
Putting on make-up, loads.

Jessie Northen (9)
Ladbrooke JMI School

The Seasons

Spring is cold and warm
There are flowerbeds under trees
In the pond there is frogspawn
And there is lots of breeze

Summer is warm and hot
You get sweaty with exercise
Remember to water your flowerpots
And in the morning the sun's going to have a fiery rise

Autumn is warm and cold
The leaves are yellow and brown
Copper and gold
All over the town

Winter is cold and freezing
Don't stand around, you'll turn to ice
Don't go out sneezing
Stay inside as warm as mice.

Benjamin Heron (9)
Ladbrooke JMI School

My Adventure

M y own secret passageway, hooray!
Y ou have to go this way.

A secret way under the ground,
D own, down and around,
V ampire bats hang from the roof,
E erie sounds abound,
N earby a light shines,
T rains so close by, they echo,
U nder the ground earth falls on you,
R escue people dig me out,
E veryone cheers when I come to the surface.

Gareth Lumb (9)
Ladbrooke JMI School

In The Garden

I was in my garden,
Playing with my neighbour,
Her cat came over the fence,
I saw it had short fur.

It jumped down in my garden,
It was standing on my plants,
I hadn't seen it before,
My neighbour said it was called Lance.

He started to walk towards me,
I thought it would've been too shy,
I tried not to look surprised,
By looking at the sky.

By this time it was 6pm,
I had to go inside very soon,
I said my goodbyes to the cat,
I went in to get my dessert and spoon.

Paul Earle (8)
Ladbrooke JMI School

My Handwriting

Me and my handwriting,
What should I do?
My teacher is coming,
'I'm after you!'

Here he comes,
Up the hallway,
Please help me,
He's approaching the doorway!

I'm going to the office,
I can feel it right now,
What, he's congratulating me,
But how?

Marcus Lilley (9)
Ladbrooke JMI School

Snow

Snow is white,
It's plain, it's cool,
No, I don't have to go to school,
We take our sledges
To the park,
Slide on our backs till it's dark,
We come home,
Shivering with cold,
Will I do this when I get old?
Dad said, 'Yes
Of course you will,'
Then sneezed and went to bed ill.

Brandon Lye (9)
Ladbrooke JMI School

Summer

The sun is shining on the beach,
Everybody's wearing shorts,
Some are playing volleyball,
Some are swimming in the sea.

But the most dazzling thing on the beach
Is the girl over there.
She has long blonde golden hair,
With eyes as blue as the sea,
She is so beautiful,
I want to go over to her.

So I do!
She suddenly looks at me,
With those blue eyes,
Then I slipped in the wet sand,
She laughed and turned away.

Edward Byrne (9)
Ladbrooke JMI School

Monster In A Cage

Monster in a cage
Full of rage
Made to dance on a stage
I wait till dark
And for a lark
I creep to the bars
I unlock the cage
And release the rage
The monster disappears into the dark.

Thomas Webb (9)
Ladbrooke JMI School

My Magic Pen

My magic pen is cool
It writes in red and blue
It didn't cost much
I got it from the zoo.

Michelle Willis (9)
Ladbrooke JMI School

Skool

School is boring
Teachers snoring
Lessons one after the other
Flicking pellets at my brother
Food is grim
In the gym
Don't be late
In getting out of the gate!

Nicolas Antoniou (9)
Ladbrooke JMI School

The Eagle

The sleek feather, the piercing eyes,
Smooth and swift the eagle flies.

Soaring, diving all the time,
His rank is prime.

Master of the skies,
With beady eyes.

His ancestors extremely wise,
Stare from the centre of his eyes.

Sam Burke (9)
Ladbrooke JMI School

The Spy Eyes

I despise spies
They are very sly
When you are in bed
They listen with gadgets
To you talking in your sleep

If you look in a spy's eye
You will see nothing
They are invisible
They live in the loft
And look at my old photos

They carry spud guns
And raid the kitchen
I wear two jumpers for protection
And a bowl on my head
Only I know they are there.

Jack McNally (9)
Ladbrooke JMI School

My Street

At number four
There is a red door

At number six
The roof is being fixed

At number eight
They have no gate

At number ten
Lives my friend Ben

At number five
There's a beehive

At number seven
They have gone to Devon

At number nine
They are all fine

This is my street
With its gardens so neat.

William Robertson-Worth (8)
Ladbrooke JMI School

My Pony

My pony she is lovely
Her name is Little Gwen
She goes galloping through the woods
Like a butterfly flying fast
Gwen you're fine
Gwen you're mine
I love you Gwen.

Beth Draper (9)
Ladbrooke JMI School

The Eagle

Flying high the eagle glides
Looking through his piercing eyes
His feathers are so sleek
As smooth as his golden beak
He waits for his prey
He swoops, grabs and flies away
King of the skies
He flies.

James Dunphy (9)
Ladbrooke JMI School

People From Around The World

Some people are mean
Some people are good
Some people like to smile
Some people should

Some people are loud and noisy
Some people are quiet
Some people have tonnes of energy
Some are always tired

Some people have smelly feet
Others are quite the same
Some people like to be cool and exciting
Some are just quite plain

Some people like to act grown-up
Some like acting as a child
Some people like to be in-between
Some act silly and wild

Some people are sensible and polite
Some don't do as asked
Some people are rude and annoying
And some eat grass!

Nevin Holness (9)
Peartree Spring Junior School

Stuck Together

In the morning,
My life is boring,
Especially when I'm stuck with you,
We always have to share the loo,
Thank heavens we're in the same class,
We can't separate like stickers and glass.
We're always partners,
When I play football, she plays football,
When we go to bed,
I'm pushed out by Ted.
Then I just stay there dangling halfway out of the bed,
You don't want a sister like mine,
Me and Ted totally stuck together all of the time.

Shanice Harwood (9)
Peartree Spring Junior School

My First Kiss!

We met in the restaurant
We went to the town
We do stuff together
We always hang around

It was your birthday
It was the best
I got you a prezzie
Mum got you a vest

We went to the market
You gave me a kiss
I looked at this boy
And he said, 'Don't diss!'

Vanessa Wyatt (10)
Peartree Spring Junior School

Inside Summer

The hot sun,
Inside the sun the yellow gleams
Inside the yellow the ice cubes melt
Inside the melting cubes the ice cream steams
Inside the steam of the ice cream the beach is quiet
Inside the quietness of the bucket and spade lay still
Inside the stillness of the bucket and spade a barbecue burns
Inside the burns of the barbecue they relax
Inside the relaxing the sun burns
Inside the sun burns it turns red
Inside the red the sky is blue
Inside the blue sky, the blue sea waves
Inside the waves they swim
Inside the swimming the flowers bloom
Inside the blooms, there's a bike
Inside the bike the sun goes down.

Jessica Fairey (9)
Peartree Spring Junior School

Life

Delivered in Bournemouth
Walked in Stepney
Talked in Chatham
Educated in Reading and Countam
Slaved in Workington
Married in Weddington
Raised family in Kidderminster
Retired in Lazenby
Pains in Ackenham
More pains in Sickinghall
Recovered in Welling
Relapsed in Illinton
Sudden death in Paston
Fell asleep in Bury.

Chrystal King (9)
Peartree Spring Junior School

My Best Friends

She taught me how
to know about the Greeks
and gave us sheets to look at

She sometimes bought us
sweets if we were good
like Haribo and boxes of jelly babies

She knew how
to make me smile
and how to make things fun

We played outside
in PE with the sun
playing hockey is fun

We went to lots of places
like the Roman baths
that was lots of fun

I love my teacher, Mrs Fordham!

Bronwen Fraser (9)
Peartree Spring Junior School

School

Lots of faces,
Shouts and yells,
Bags and books
And ringing bells.

Pens and pencils,
Boards and chalk,
PE, singing,
Lots of talk.

'Line up quietly,
What's the rule?'
Add these up
They equal *school!*

Leigh-Ellen Caton (10)
Peartree Spring Junior School

Hey Baby

Listen as the baby utters a soft cry
like a little chick's chirp.

Feel the baby's little button nose,
it's as soft as melted chocolate.

Know how it feels for the baby's hand
to wrap around your little finger.

Hear the baby's bare feet
tiptoe across the floor.

Stroke the baby's small hairless head,
it's as smooth as its bottom.

Look at the baby's chubby cheeks
that are as hot as lava when it wakes from a peaceful sleep.

Aema Watson (10)
Peartree Spring Junior School

School Is Cool

School is cool
Don't be a fool
Work all day
Then it's play
When lunch is here
We all give a big cheer
Then it's time to
Do some sports
In our shorts
When it's time
To go home
We always moan.

Charlotte Clarkson Barrett (10)
Peartree Spring Junior School

At The Beach

At the beach
People were playing
At the beach
Seagulls were screeching

At the beach
Children were buying ice creams
At the beach
People were having dreams

At the beach
Children were paddling in the sea
At the beach
And a little girl fell over and cut her knee

At the beach
People were very hot
At the beach
Adults were holding ice cream pots

At the beach
People have packed up and gone home
At the beach
Everyone has cleared out of the busy beach.

Amy Brown (11)
Peartree Spring Junior School

My Best Friend!

He knows when I am down
Because I wear a frown
When I am down

He taught me how to talk
About him of course
But I didn't mind cos I loved him

We went to lots of places
We travelled all around
Until he moved away, I don't see him now

He bought me cuddly toys
And lots of squidgy things
Because I loved cuddling things
Including him

We played board games
Like snakes and ladders
He used to always win

He knows when I am happy
My smile goes across my face
Especially when I see him

My brother's great!

Emily Lambert (9)
Peartree Spring Junior School

My Best Friend

He taught me how to draw
Disney pictures
Like the Little Mermaid, Flounder
And an angelfish
Using a grid

He knows everything there is to know
About famous people and their life
Like Vicky and Spencer from EastEnders
Are actually going out

He visits places I've
Always wanted to see
Like Australia and maybe America
But I'm not sure if he's been to America

I tell him secrets
About who I love
Because I trust him
With my secrets and
Sometimes my life

He's the greatest uncle in the world
Because he's my Uncle Matt.

Ellen Forster (8)
Peartree Spring Junior School

The Cat In The Hat

I'm the cat in the hat,
My hat is red and white,
I'm happy, jolly and bright.

I'm the cat in the hat,
My whiskers are as long as snakes,
I like to eat fish and cakes.

I'm the cat in the hat,
I have sharp claws but I will not scratch,
They grab my fish for me to catch.

I'm the cat in the hat,
I am hairy,
But don't be afraid,
I'm not scary.

I'm the cat in the hat,
I'll be your friend,
Until now, I must go but my happiness
Is what I will send
To you.

Connor Gordon (7)
Peartree Spring Junior School

Flowers

Flowers in the garden
Flowers in the park
How they love the sunshine
But definitely not the dark

Lots of different colours
Lots of different smells
My favourite flower of them all
Are the beautiful bluebells

Flowers are not just pretty
They have a job to do
When you're feeling sick and ill
They can help cure you

So when you see a flower
Sitting on its own
Please don't pull it out of the ground
It's much better in its own home.

Lauren Phipps (8)
Peartree Spring Junior School

Birds

Birds are sweet
And they're neat,
They perch on a branch with
Their little feet.
I love their chatter
And their beautiful singing
Especially the robin on a
Christmas morning.

Holly Morton (8)
Peartree Spring Junior School

My Best Friend

She cared for me
Bought me toys
Rocked me to sleep
While singing lullabies

She burnt the sausages
Burgers too
Taught me how to bake cakes
Burnt them too

She knew what I liked
But now she's gone
Died in a hospital bed
She couldn't hear some things I said

We sometimes stood in the back garden
Feeding the birds
Went for a walk in the woods
Fed the squirrels lots of nuts

My mum was my best friend.

Chris Patterson (10)
Peartree Spring Junior School

Tiger, Tiger

Tiger, tiger running loose
Over there is a lonely moose
Hunt it down as your prey
That will be your dinner today

Tiger, tiger feeling down
Wondering if you would wear a crown
Kill the lion under the sun
Like you're playing, having fun

Tiger, tiger on the throne
Now it's yours and yours to own
Sitting under a tall green tree
Now you're happy to be free.

Tommy Hatt (9)
Peartree Spring Junior School

Poem About Tutankhamun

There was a boy called Tutankhamun
He lived in Egypt then he died and he got buried in a tomb
This man who was crowned king when he was only eight
Everyone thinks he was murdered by his aids
In Egypt you can see a mask through a piece of glass
You can also see all his belongings from his past.

Ross Jenkins (9)
Peartree Spring Junior School

Calm Places

I love calm places,
Where peace is all around
And all your thoughts
Are left alone.

The sound of mellow,
The scent of love,
With a touch of floating,
While your heart is thumping.

The glorious murmur,
The wonderful flowing,
The marvellous stillness,
All sprinkled on top.

It's a cushion of comfort,
A soft solution,
With a bubbly blanket,
All rolled into one.

That's why I love
Calm places.

Georgia Lansbury (11)
Peartree Spring Junior School

The Rules That Rule The School

Only speak when you're spoken to,
Don't stand and grin like a fool,
Pay attention or risk a detention,
We're the rules that rule the school.

Hands must not be in pockets,
When addressing a member of staff,
Though smiling is sometimes permitted,
You need written permission to laugh.

Boys must stand to attention
And salute when they pass the head,
Girls are expected to curtsey
And lower their eyes instead.

Sit up straight, do as you're told,
If you want to come top of the class,
Bribes must be paid in cash,
if you want to be sure to pass.

Charlie Marvell (8)
Peartree Spring Junior School

Go You Fierce Fighter

The fierce fighter is as fast as a second,
The fierce fighter never gives up,
The fierce fighter has its ways,
The fierce fighter, the fierce fighter.

The fierce fighter has a spotty coat,
The fierce fighter is no joke,
The fierce fighter has one prey,
The fierce fighter, the fierce fighter.

The fierce fighter is no friend,
The fierce fighter plays no games,
The fierce fighter is colours of brown and black,
The fierce fighter is the cheetah.

Natalie Wall (9)
SS Alban & Stephen RC JMI School, St Albans

We Must Save The Sea!

We must save the sea,
The watery waves are as clear as can be!
Yet humans decide to ruin this beauty,
They pollute the sea, honestly!
They throw in their rubbish without a care in the world,
Yet lovely creatures this beauty does hold!
Bits of paper, sticks and a can,
The sea looks disgraceful against the sand!
But we can sort out this problem, you know,
We just need the world to show
That this is a wonderful place for creatures to be,
So please don't pollute the sea!
We must save the sea,
The watery waves are as clear as can be!
Yet humans decide to ruin this beauty,
They pollute the sea, honestly!

Lauren Cesena (10)
SS Alban & Stephen RC JMI School, St Albans

Slitherer The Snake

The king of reptiles
Rustles through the leaves - slitherer

The one whose tongue
Is a poisonous dart - slitherer

The vicious venom of this viper
Shall poison your immune system

Although its skin looks beautiful
Like a patterned Axminster
Don't be fooled for he
Attacks like a lion
Stings like a bee.

Makoye Kampengele (10)
SS Alban & Stephen RC JMI School, St Albans

I Wanna Cake!

Four current buns in a baker's shop,
Big and round, quite plump on top.

Then in came a boy with some money one day,
His hair was as thick and as yellow as hay.

He said to the baker, 'I'm hungry you see,
So why don't you give them all to me?'

The baker said, 'You're far too fat,
I'd rather feed them to my cat.'

The boy looked down, looking for his toes,
But the smell of baking was right up his nose!

'But I want a cake; I must have one now!
I have the money, I sold our cow.

I have enough money to buy the shop.'
But the baker said, 'No, no you must stop!

Does your mother know you're here?'
'No, no, I sold *her* last year!'

Casey-Drew Williams (10)
SS Alban & Stephen RC JMI School, St Albans

Stop Polluting The Sea

Stop polluting the sea, you're killing all the seals,
Stop polluting the sea, you're poisoning the fishes' meals,
Stop polluting the sea, you're hurting the lobsters' claws,
Stop polluting the sea, you're breaking all the laws.

Stop polluting the sea, you're putting lives at risk,
Stop polluting the sea, you're gonna get found out on disk,
Stop polluting the sea, you're gonna get lots of blackmail,
Stop polluting the sea, you're gonna get sent to jail.

Lauren Murphy (10)
SS Alban & Stephen RC JMI School, St Albans

Deadly Enemy

Killer, killer, killer,
Hear that roar, roar, roar,
The scalding flame,
Enemy of St George,
Deadly, daring dragon,
Colours like traffic lights,
Eyes as big as roundabouts,
Hear that roar, roar, roar,
Killer, killer, killer.

Victims, victims, victims,
Hear that crunch, crunch, crunch,
The sneaky cat burglar,
The roaster of boys,
Deadly, daring dragon,
Girl gobbler,
Dude diner,
Hear that crunch, crunch, crunch,
Victims, victims, victims.

Helen Easton (10)
SS Alban & Stephen RC JMI School, St Albans

Lion

I'm the lion, I'm the lion
I'm the fierce-looking lion
I'm the Devil, Devil the lion

They say I'm sly, fast, brave and strong
I'm the king, king of Africa
I'm Devil, Devil the lion

They say my eyes are like fire
My roar is like a tornado
My mane is as bushy as a tree in spring

That's me Devil, Devil the lion.

Bridget McDonagh (9)
SS Alban & Stephen RC JMI School, St Albans

There's Something New In The Water

The fishes are looking drowsy, whales are drifting down,
Crabs are dying and birds are going brown,
Something is melting the water, people will have to slaughter,
There is something in the water that makes fishes bleed,
It makes the sharks drain and it flows upon the seas.

There's something new in the water.
There's something new in the water
And it's making cancer spread.

It comes from ships and the cities, flows upon the world,
Making animals suffer,
Slaughter,
Slaughter,
Slaughter,
It makes people cough,
People are dying, animals are dying,
There's something new in the water.

Joseph Baker (10)
SS Alban & Stephen RC JMI School, St Albans

They Did It

Sometimes it leapt from up above,
Sometimes it crept and killed the dove,
Sometimes it's a horrible sight,
Sometimes it gives you a fright.

They started it,
They started it.

It comes down from the highest hill,
It comes down wanting to kill,
It comes from the biggest forest,
It tries to kill my kids, honest.

They're killing, they're killing,
They're killing us!

Alice Colwill (9) & Eleanor Baker (10)
SS Alban & Stephen RC JMI School, St Albans

Pure Murder

There's something there in the water,
It's neither thin nor fat,
It's not the fish's fault,
It brings sickness,
It brings death,
The oil tankers are sinking,
With their oil everywhere,
It sticks to birds' wings,
Making them drown to death,
It's driving the fish crazy,
Then putting them to death.

The cars are producing,
That dirty old air,
It affects the water,
It affects the air,
More humans need to think,
About this murder,
It's pure murder, it's pure murder, murder, murder,
It's truly pure murder, murder, murder.

Jonathan Roche (10)
SS Alban & Stephen RC JMI School, St Albans

Yu-Gi-Oh Card

Children buying
Parents sighing
Children trading
Others playing
Children fighting
Teachers telling
Head teachers banning
Children moaning.

Celeste Hartley (9)
SS Alban & Stephen RC JMI School, St Albans

Hedgy The Hedgehog

Hedgy the hedgehog eats worms and slugs,
Hedgy the hedgehog is a spiky creature,
Hedgy the hedgehog curls up in a ball, oh that hedgehog in a hedge.

Never been to the hospital tiggy-winkles,
Never been run over by any old car,
Never been to visit the Queen, oh that hedgehog in a hedge.

Timid as a baby duck,
Spiky as a holly bush,
Smiles like a little girl,
Curling up in the cold of winter.

Always sleeps through the cold of winter,
Always been the colour brown,
Always been able to bath himself, oh that hedgehog in a hedge.

Dreamed he could go around the world,
Dreamed he was a porcupine,
Dreamed he was in a luxurious place, oh that hedgehog in a hedge.

Timid as a baby duck,
Spiky as a holly bush,
Smiles like a little girl,
Curling up in the cold of winter.

Elizabeth Colton (10)
SS Alban & Stephen RC JMI School, St Albans

If Stars Were Fish

If fish were stars
And stars were fish
In river night sky
Lights would swish.

Nancy Singleton (8)
SS Alban & Stephen RC JMI School, St Albans

The Tiger

Tiger, his claws are meat hooks
His teeth are as shiny as ice
You would be dead if he takes a bite

His paws are soft, shaggy slippers
His skin is as smooth as leather
His eyes glisten in the evening sun
And in the hot weather

He pounces on his prey
Rips its skin off
And eats it for his dinner
He does it again so he can get fuller

Running through the jungle
Nothing in the way
Speeding from the poachers
Who would kill him today.

Liam Ryan (10)
SS Alban & Stephen RC JMI School, St Albans

Tiger

Tiger, tiger,
So, so fierce,
Tiger, tiger,
Orange black coat,
Fur flaming in the night,
Tiger, tiger,
Roars like a fierce dragon,
Tiger, tiger
Teeth like silver-white,
Tiger, tiger
An eating machine,
Oh that tiger!

Vincenzo Davino (10)
SS Alban & Stephen RC JMI School, St Albans

Sly Snake

Sly snake slowly slithering towards its prey,
Sly snake able to go all the way,
Sly snake as long as a skyscraper sideways,
Sly snake, its tail would get lost in a maze.

Sly snake can swallow you all in one piece,
Sly snake I'd be scared of his poisonous teeth,
Sly snake I would call him a stealthy thief,
Sly snake enjoys a good piece of meat.

Sly snake teeth like the sharpest knife,
Sly snake, be careful of your mice,
Sly snake definitely a muddy predator,
Sly snake it will chop you slice by slice.

Anna Foxall (10)
SS Alban & Stephen RC JMI School, St Albans

The Dead Sea

The whale didn't do it,
The swordfish didn't do it,
The hammerhead didn't do it,
As the waves pass by.

The clownfish didn't do it,
The shark didn't do it,
The seahorse didn't do it,
Anyway they all will die.

The manta ray didn't do it,
The seagull didn't do it,
I know who did it,
The humans killed the sea.

Nicolas De Bellis (10)
SS Alban & Stephen RC JMI School, St Albans

Peter Python

The quick-striking foe
That attacks anything that moves
Its swift and sturdy nature
Attacks nothing that moos

The creature of darkness
A killer of birds
Lurks in the forest
Slithers in dirt

Strikes like a spider
Feeds on prey
Can even eat lions
In the month of May

The hiss of his voice
Scares wolves in the dark
One of his attacks cost him
One long red mark.

Shaquille Trotman (9)
SS Alban & Stephen RC JMI School, St Albans

Autumn Leaves

Red, yellow, brown, orange
Beautiful colours that I see
Spinning around and touching the ground
Little leaves dying, big leaves dying
Jump into piles, stack them up
Watching the rain over and over again
Jumping in puddles, splashing about
Picking up leaves, soon they'll be gone.

Taisha Pickering (9)
SS Alban & Stephen RC JMI School, St Albans

Gorilla!

I'm a gorilla
As tough as roars
I'm very hairy
I'm a growling gorilla with my
Gigantic growl
Like a human in a big bath towel
I'm as big as a door
My favourite food are bananas
I can always make some room for more
I'm going to get you
I'm going to get you
Rrrooaarr!

Michaella Rios (9)
SS Alban & Stephen RC JMI School, St Albans

Slowly

Slowly the world turns around
Slowly you touch the ground
Slowly the man makes a tile
Slowly the snail slithers a mile

Slowly the shepherd herds his flock
Slowly Dad fixes the clock
Slowly William plays football
Slowly Mum goes to the mall.

Harriet Tickel (8)
St Dominic RC JMI Primary School, Harpenden

The Elephants

Doodling on the side of my page,
Thinking about a poem,
When it suddenly hit me,
What about an elephant?
Big, scary and very hairy,
Its trunk a long, twisted pipe,
Its tusks as strong as diamonds,
But used by poachers,
Unfortunately sold as keys.

Oliver Constant (11)
St Dominic RC JMI Primary School, Harpenden

Spitfire

Soaring up and down between the clouds,
turning, spinning, twisting round,
bullets fire like deadly knives,
stamps resembling human lives.
A metal eagle soaring down,
terrorising streets and towns,
brown and green grease-lightning flies,
over wrecks where bodies lie,
over fields and trees and lakes,
fumes spurt out like long black snakes,
fields like patchwork, roads like wire.
It is the deadly *spitfire!*

James Mottram (11)
St Dominic RC JMI Primary School, Harpenden

Dragon

(Inspired by Christopher Paloni)

A beast of the land and sky,
Hear its shrill and terrifying cry,
It breathes a flame of blinding light,
That illuminates even the darkest night,
Through the mountains upon high,
The beast roars its freedom to the skies,
It flies and flies for miles around,
Until it comes to rest upon the ground.

William Tickel (11)
St Dominic RC JMI Primary School, Harpenden

Wild Horse

Inside the horse's eye,
the black button.
Inside the black button,
the horse's teeth.
Inside the horse's teeth,
the lump of snow.
Inside the lump of snow,
the horse's tongue.
Inside the horse's tongue,
the blood of a bug.
Inside the blood of a bug,
the dirty lake.
Inside the dirty lake,
the horse's leg.
Inside the horse's leg,
the dark forest.
Inside the dark forest,
the horse's hoof.
Inside the horse's hoof,
the grey sky.
Inside the grey sky,
the horse's eye.

Louise Spicer (10)
St Dominic RC JMI Primary School, Harpenden

The Bear's Paw

Inside the bear's paw, a human's hand,
Inside the human's hand, the bear's claw,
Inside the bear's claw, the fish's scales,
Inside the fish's scales, the bear's teeth,
Inside the bear's teeth, the blood of a fish,
Inside the blood of a fish, the air of the forest,
Inside the air of the forest, the smoke of a fire,
Inside the smoke of a fire, the smell of fish,
Inside the smell of fish, the bear's paw.

Paul O'Brien (11)
St Dominic RC JMI Primary School, Harpenden

Golden Daffodils

Frilly yellow trumpets give off sweet scent;
tall strong stem reaches high;
waxy texture, soft to touch;
crispy brown sepals like delicate wings.

Golden flowers like lovely medals,
glowing by the sunset,
blowing in the wind,

climbing to the clouds of the heavens.

Hannah Atton (11)
St Dominic RC JMI Primary School, Harpenden

Fire's End

While fire blazes
In a field of daisies
An epic fight was fought
When a damsel was caught

Between dragon and knight
It went on through the night
Then with a final stroke
The dragon's life was broke.

Dominic Fox (11)
St Dominic RC JMI Primary School, Harpenden

Daffodils

They sway in the sunlight in waves of gold
And yellow, colourful and frilly yet strong
And still, their frilly trumpets play music
In the air and smell as sweet as perfume
In a wonderful sea of daffodils.

Kate Allinson (10)
St Dominic RC JMI Primary School, Harpenden

The King Of The Jungle

Inside the lion's roar, a big dark cave,
Inside the big dark cave, glistening teeth,
Inside the glistening teeth, the prey of the lion,
Inside the prey of the lion, a confident pounce,
Inside the confident pounce, the wind in the lion's mane,
Inside the wind in the lion's mane, its sun-coloured fur,
Inside its sun-coloured fur, its gentle eyes,
Inside it's gentle eyes, a lion's roar.

Emily Wigley (11)
St Dominic RC JMI Primary School, Harpenden

Chameleon

Inside the chameleon's eye, the jungle heat,
Inside the jungle heat, the chameleon's long tongue,
Inside the chameleon's long tongue, the green twisting creepers,
Inside the green twisting creepers, the chameleon's rough scaly skin,
Inside the chameleon's rough scaly skin, the buzzing of mosquitoes,
Inside the buzzing mosquitoes, the chameleon's eye.

Matthew Heyes (11)
St Dominic RC JMI Primary School, Harpenden

Springtime Magic

The lush scent of spring,
Flowers bursting through the ground,
Fills the air with magic,
A feeling rarely found.

For if you've seen a bud open
And watched it grow and grow,
You'd know what magic feels like,
With all its colours aglow.

The first steps of a lamb,
Or the first bud of spring,
Blossom spreading like fire,
Upon the trees, now pink.

I look across the moors,
Purple with sweet-smelling heather,
Little fox cubs playing,
Rolling and fighting together.

Little fledglings' first flight,
Each starting to get their own feathers,
Springtime magic will last forever,
. . . and ever,
. . . and ever,
. . . and ever.

Jessica Maberly (11)
St Dominic RC JMI Primary School, Harpenden

Proudly

Proudly the sun shows off her light,
Proudly the owl hoots loudly in the night,
Proudly the king shows off his might,
Proudly the knight shows off how he fights.

Catherine Geraghty (9)
St Dominic RC JMI Primary School, Harpenden

Gently

Gently Thierry Henry pots the ball in the net
Gently the men shook hands when they met
Gently the mum holds her daughter's hand
Gently the man tapped the drum in the band

Gently a man shoots a ball
Gently the lady catches the cake
Gently the sister helped the baby
Gently a man hit the ball with the bat.

Francesca Berry (9)
St Dominic RC JMI Primary School, Harpenden

Rapidly

Rapidly the cheetah sprints across the land,
Rapidly Thierry Henry scores against Tim Howard,
Rapidly Lehman dives for the ball,
Rapidly a shooting star crosses the sky.

Joshua Higham (9)
St Dominic RC JMI Primary School, Harpenden

Proudly

Proudly the rhino crosses the plain
Proudly the lion lifts its head
Proudly the tortoise follows the path
Proudly the shark guards its territory.

Adam O'Hagan (8)
St Dominic RC JMI Primary School, Harpenden

Angrily

Angrily the wind cries through the trees,
Angrily the tides zoom in from the sea,
Angrily the warrior stabs his opponent,
Angrily thunder booms from the sky.

Angrily the lion roars from his cage,
Angrily the lady threw tomatoes on the stage,
Angrily the eagle pecked the man's face,
Angrily the bull takes back a pace.

Rosie Doyle (8)
St Dominic RC JMI Primary School, Harpenden

Gracefully

Gracefully the zebras run in a line.
Gracefully the blackbird flies in the sunshine.
Gracefully the afternoon breeze fills the sky.
Gracefully an aeroplane flies so high.
Gracefully the beautiful birds sing a song.
Gracefully the drummer tapped his drum.
Gracefully the flame blows out.
Gracefully the clouds move about.

Emma Gurney (8)
St Dominic RC JMI Primary School, Harpenden

Bravely

Bravely a boy saved somebody's life.
Bravely a man fights a tiger.
Bravely an army of men go to war.
Bravely Roy Keane scores the winning goal.

Bravely somebody jumped off a cliff onto the other side.
Bravely somebody had a sword fight.
Bravely a man swam past a shark.
Bravely somebody dodged a cannonball.

Ashwell Phillips (8)
St Dominic RC JMI Primary School, Harpenden

Sadly

Sadly the woeful man walks from his wife's grave
Sadly the robbed woman went to the police
Sadly the homeless boy walked away from the orphanage
Sadly the baby deer trotted away from her dead mother.

Joseph D'Arcy (9)
St Dominic RC JMI Primary School, Harpenden

Bravely

Bravely the warrior rides into battle.
Bravely the captain steers his ship through the storm.
Bravely the skier shoots down the slope.
Bravely the cormorant dives for his fish.

Michael Patten (9)
St Dominic RC JMI Primary School, Harpenden

Quickly

Quickly the dolphin jumped out of the water and back in.
Quickly the plane landed in Berlin.
Quickly the ballerina did a pirouette in the air.
Quickly the film star brushed her hair.

Quickly a squirrel ran away.
Quickly a lion pounced on its prey.
Quickly the girl drank her drink.
Quickly the professional ice skater skates on the local ice rink.

Charlotte D'Ancey (9)
St Dominic RC JMI Primary School, Harpenden

Skilfully

Skilfully Van Nistelrooy scores a perfect goal,
Skilfully Paul Scoles dribbles round the Arsenal defender,
Skilfully the Formula 1 goes round the corner,
Skilfully the artist does his painting.

Abigail Smith (9)
St Dominic RC JMI Primary School, Harpenden

Purposefully

Purposefully the duck races for the bread,
Purposefully the rugby player doesn't pass but runs instead
Purposefully the adult grasps his purse
Purposefully the goddess unleashes her curse

Purposefully the bishop declares his speech
Purposefully the child defends his peach
Purposefully the civilian remembers his change
Purposefully the lion destroys his cage.

Roderick Cox (8)
St Dominic RC JMI Primary School, Harpenden

Gracefully

Gracefully Van Nistelrooy dribbles passed Arsenal's defender.
Gracefully the wind whistles through the leaves.
Gracefully the swan uncurls its beautiful neck.
Gracefully the ballerina twirls on the stage.

Alice Duddy (9)
St Dominic RC JMI Primary School, Harpenden

Slowly

Slowly the rabbit nibbles some hay
Slowly the snail slithers away
Slowly the clock chimes nine
Slowly the passengers wait at the railway line

Slowly the collie sneaks downstairs
Slowly the goalie saves the goal
Slowly the man lies down for a nap
Slowly the artist finishes a picture.

Hannah Dodd (8)
St Dominic RC JMI Primary School, Harpenden

Proudly

Proudly the prince takes the throne
Proudly Crespo takes the goal
Proudly I open a new shop
Proudly I'm walking up the aisle to be knighted by the Queen

Proudly a father holds his son
Proudly the new classroom is opened
Proudly the 100m champion wins the race
Proudly they sing their new song.

Charlotte Hart (9)
St Dominic RC JMI Primary School, Harpenden

Rapidly

Rapidly the world's best explorer travels around the world
Rapidly the ball curved into the right hand corner
Rapidly a rugby player scores a winning try
Rapidly meteors shoot across the sky.

Joseph Wigley (9)
St Dominic RC JMI Primary School, Harpenden

Accurately

Accurately Murphy scores.
Accurately Bond kills Goldfinger.
Accurately Ronaldiniho passes it to Kluivert
Accurately Crocodile Dundee defeats a crocodile

Accurately Robinson scores a try
Accurately Legolas gets a bull's eye
Accurately Dudek saves a penalty kick
Accurately England win!

Charlie Roberts (9)
St Dominic RC JMI Primary School, Harpenden

Teachers

Some are boring,
Some are great,
Some are like fisherman
And pick you as their bait.

Some are groovy,
Some are fine,
But my class teacher
Is totally sublime.

Gillian Whitworth (10)
St Dominic RC JMI Primary School, Harpenden

The Lion's Eye

Inside the lion's eyes, blue sea water,
Inside the blue sea water, the lion's water
Inside the lion's water, the lion's sharp teeth
Inside the lion's sharp teeth, blades from swords
Inside the blades from swords, the lion's golden fur
Inside the lion's golden fur, crisp leaves
Inside the crisp leaves, rain water,
Inside the rain water, the lion's eyes.

Marcus Ibberson (10)
St Dominic RC JMI Primary School, Harpenden

Spooks In The Night

I get into bed
Turn off my lamp
Then it all goes dark

The wind is howling
Ghostly shadows come out from inside my wardrobe
The figures lurk towards me in rhythm with the tap dripping

I lie there restless
As I turn the floorboards creak
I close my eye and try to hide

The clock strikes twelve
Then on turns the silence
And then the thoughts creep into mind

I hear a voice
A cold shiver runs down my back
But finally I get to sleep.

Amy D'Arcy (10)
St Dominic RC JMI Primary School, Harpenden

Hear Me

Roll of thunder hear my cry,
Strike of lightning see me die,
Stand alone, stand in fear,
It is your voice which led me here.

Sun of power stand apart,
Moon of darkness don't depart,
Looking on in midnight walk,
Listen for the endless talk.

Stars above shine bright and clear,
Water running the endless tear,
I fought once I'll fight again,
If it will stop this endless pain.

Katie Reimann (11)
St Dominic RC JMI Primary School, Harpenden

Daffodils

Over the hill, what did I see?
But a field of daffodils
Beautiful and golden
With heads like wonderful trumpets
With petals like glowing flames
A wonderful carpet of yellow
The flowers swishing like waves out on the open sea
With stems like coral under the yellow ocean.

George Finch (11)
St Dominic RC JMI Primary School, Harpenden

Noises In The Night

I go to bed, I hear the baby bawling
The darkness is calling
The light is falling
The wind is roaring
My dad is snoring
The wolves are shrieking
Floorboards creaking
The night is back
The sky is black
The ghosts creeping round with a big grey sack
Owls hooting
Hunters shooting
The moon hangs bright
In the pitch-black night
Boxes rattling
Windows shattering
The clouds are gone
The moon is out
As white as a swan
The ghosts are about.

Fergus Cox (9)
St Dominic RC JMI Primary School, Harpenden

The Ant

I was walking through the long, sharp grass
When I saw a giant
The earth started to shake
I ran for my life
Then I appeared by an ocean!
A slimy green toad crashed down next to me
Looking like an ugly monster.

Nick Clift (10)
St John Fisher RC Primary School, St Albans

The Squirrel

I twist and turn as I jump branch to branch,
Like a rhythmic gym ribbon flying through the air,
My paws touch the bumpy, hard branch,
I scrape my claws in,
I fall, luckily I land on my feet so I will start again,
I climb up the big giant,
I climb up and start once more.

Joe Dwyer (10)
St John Fisher RC Primary School, St Albans

A Day In The Life Of Sean, The Hedgehog

I woke up, it was night
Then all of a sudden the scary noises gave me a fright
There was grass all over the place
It was like a never-ending maze

I carried on walking and fell off the path
It was as if I had fallen off a cliff
Noise of the animals scare me off
I feel like I am being watched.

Christopher Samways (10)
St John Fisher RC Primary School, St Albans

The Blade Of Grass

The blade of grass is as big as the blue sky,
It is as tall as the houses in the town,
All of them together stand like a row of school children.

The flower is as tall as a mountain peak,
It smells just like sap dropping out of the stem,
The petals are as bright as the yellow sun.

The tree is as tall as the mountain K2,
The leaves are as smooth as my armour or shell,
It waves in the wind like a Mexican wave.

Alexandra Rukin (10)
St John Fisher RC Primary School, St Albans

Foraging For Food

I've come from under the stone to the world
And I find myself faced with an enormous puddle,
Looming like an ocean in front of me.
Dare I cross the log
Leading to a never-ending forest the other side?

I go across, shuddering to think that I may fall to the sea
And I now see the forest all around me.
There is the sun shining through as the petals fall off.

I now find out it is a thing called a dandelion
And some flying mechanisms are up ahead,
As some propellers fly past me.

I climb up a woody surface,
Which is like, what humans call,
The size of two Empire State Buildings,
As a caterpillar scuttles past.

As I end my forage for food,
I am faced with a task,
To cross the sea on a boat,
I've made it! I climb up a wall and slide on ice -
Now I've got to make it back!

Gemma Hollman (10)
St John Fisher RC Primary School, St Albans

The Forest

F ire-shaped leaves blow along the floor,
O ver-sized toadstools like an umbrella,
R unning up the wall is a large vine,
E normous thorn bush like a load of pins,
S trange and furry moss on the wall,
T housands of sticks sleeping on the mud.

Kieran Neville (10)
St John Fisher RC Primary School, St Albans

Pond And Grassy

The pond gleams like a mirror reflecting the sky,
The grass is so green as the slimy worms go around,
The birds jump, whistle and fly,
The scary insects crawl in the ground.

See the grass standing in a row all straight,
Feel the pond shiver and shake with frogs jumping out,
The daisies and dandelions dance and shake,
Hear the squirrels making rustling noises like leaves shaking about.

Fabiola Di Gesaro (10)
St John Fisher RC Primary School, St Albans

The Summer Day

The blades of grass, like a mountain of green,
The yellow and gold leaves are like the sun on a sunny day,
The flies and bees buzzing about,
The soft sweet-smelling flowers wafting in the breeze,
The trees rustling in the cool wind,
The white clouds like cotton wool floating about,
The blossom, pink and white like jewels set into a green necklace,
The buttercups are butter melting in the sun,
The birds whistling in the soft green leaves.

Elizabeth Smyth (10)
St John Fisher RC Primary School, St Albans

Life As An Ant

I'm an ant walking round our school field,
I'm sinking in wet mud, like quicksand,
Tall, thin blades of grass, like huge trees,
A gust of wind has lifted me up,
It was like a tornado blowing me away,
I am now floating in our school pond.

Conor O'Malley-Jump (10)
St John Fisher RC Primary School, St Albans

The Thorn Bush

The thorn bush is a spider city,
Millions of spiders dwell there.
It is a maze of webs,
Shimmering in the sun.

A small stream of light,
Lights up the city.
The yellow flowers on top
Are like gardens for the spiders.

The sharp thorns protect the webs,
The rough and smooth leaves
Decorate the city with their
Beautiful colours of greens.

Yet this city remains a secret,
Alone in a field,
Left untouched,
Until man destroys it forever.

Catherine Chapman (10)
St John Fisher RC Primary School, St Albans

The Ant's View Of Trees

It is like a forest
Which is very big
I see a huge giant
Which is very near
It has a vicious bird
Which is black and rough
It has a huge coat
Which is green and smooth
It has loads of arms
Which have hundreds of fingers
It has hundreds of pimples
Which are all over its body
Then I run as fast as I can.

Niall Quigley (10)
St John Fisher RC Primary School, St Albans

The Plain

I'm a squirrel in a tree
And I see not very much because of the branches,
I can see a hill, I can see a field like a plain of grass,
I can just see flickers of sunlight,
Far away I see a tree as tall as a mountain
And a pond sparkling like a lake.

The leaves fall on the ground like crisps,
I see all the blossom all over the floor,
I can see glimpses of other birds in the lake.

Lewis Gaffney (10)
St John Fisher RC Primary School, St Albans

Bird's Point Of View

It's like a jungle up here,
I can't get out,
Help me, my wing is stuck,
These green things smell nice,
I want to know what they are.

I can see the light,
I must be nearly out,
That's good, I can see clearly.

Enzo Carini (10)
St John Fisher RC Primary School, St Albans

The Spider

S piders see dandelions as huge umbrellas on sticks,
P eople are sometimes scared of them because of their legs,
I nsects and flies are their favourite food,
D ead flies and dead wasps all over its web,
E very type of spider has eight legs,
R unning is impossible, I'll have a feast.

Aaron Watts (10)
St John Fisher RC Primary School, St Albans

The Storm

The wrinkled bark feels hot upon my legs,
I scurry up a tree, the ground looms in my face.
I reach the very tip top,
I stand proudly on top of the skyscraper.
Branches claw at me like hands,
The pond surrounds me like a mirror.
Dropped carelessly into the ground,
I look to the sky, white flakes surround me,
A great snake of lightning suddenly lashes out,
Electric and powerful.

I run as fast as a cheetah,
The field is a lake.
Sticks bob up and down,
Heavy drops of water almost drown me.
The flower heads drip, their colour draining,
Birds circle overhead like hawks.
Watching, waiting,
Like a frog I jump to lowest branch.
Leaves fall, they are bricks,
Falling so fast from my skyscraper.

The lake spreads so fast, so quick,
Like an everlasting blanket of darkness.
It hugs me, choking me,
Flowers fall thick and fast.
Petals drip, drop, drip,
The once green field has turned into a swamp.
The lake turns into a raging sea,
Waves toss and turn!
Then . . . silence, the storm has stopped,
The day returns.

Bethany Jakubowski (10)
St John Fisher RC Primary School, St Albans

The Fox

The trees loom like monsters all around me,
But I am not scared.
I'm stuck in some deserted place,
But I am not scared.
There is a giant right behind me,
But I am not scared.
There is a huge brown sea ahead of me,
But I am not scared.
There is no hope,
But I'm still not scared.

But what is this?
There is shouting as loud as music,
Giants rampage through the foresty floor,
With a mass of weapons.
The ash is dancing in the dark night,
They are still following me.
I can see a hound sniffing, hiding in leaves,
I turn around to the sparkling fire,
The men are still rampaging at me.

Now I'm scared!

Thomas Pugh (10)
St John Fisher RC Primary School, St Albans

Ant's Point Of View

All the trees look like two big giants put together,
For as far as I can see there is a never-ending forest,
The yellow dandelions are like the big bright sun
Shining its bright light on me.
The puddles are like a really long sea that drifts all day,
The fallen leaves provide boats to ride on all day long,
The sticks in the water are like canoes that you can drift away on,
The cut grass is like mountains of flaky snow,
The flies are like big aeroplanes flying over my head.

Emily Campbell (9)
St John Fisher RC Primary School, St Albans

The Enchanted Corner

The enchanted corner is magic
There is sticky weed as sticky as glue
There is blossom like wintry white snow

The thorns are as sharp as razor blades
Potholes are the entrances to secret underground caves

The moss is damp like a wet patch of grass
The enchanted tree is growing like a giant
The fallen grass covering an entrance

The silver bars like a jail
You are always wondering if the trees are peering down at you
The grass is a huge forest where you can look at the canopy.

Rory Lysaght (9)
St John Fisher RC Primary School, St Albans

The Life Of A Bird

The breeze blowing against my face
as I fly in the sky.
The sun shining like a diamond
placed there in the sky.
I go down from the sky
to look for worms to take to my chicks for a meal.
I pick a couple and spread my wings
and fly into the open sky.
I fly through the tree
like a missile.
I dodge all the branches
and finally make it to my nest.

Jak Hamilton (9)
St John Fisher RC Primary School, St Albans

The Midnight Tree

I'm on a tree which looks like a jungle,
The leaves are eyes staring at me from high above,
Like a diving board so high, leaves jump off it,
The layer of grass looks like an ocean which I'm lost in.
The monster's arms grabbing things in the night,
Like a cave so dark, people walk past it,
There are loads of gaps so I can see the midnight sky.

Amber McShane (9)
St John Fisher RC Primary School, St Albans

The Green Grass

The blades of grass are like fins of green sharks,
Popping out of the brown sea,
A mist of green with yellow clouds,
The colour of the sunshine.
I can hear the rustle of green leaves
As the wind blows,
Smell the scent of bright yellow clouds,
I feel the blades of the grass,
Tickling me like fingers.

Stephanie Quinn (10)
St John Fisher RC Primary School, St Albans

The Adventure Day For An Ant

The pond, a wide never-ending sea,
A dandelion, a huge umbrella,
The roots, a mountain of adventure,
The daisies, a never-ending colour.
The trees, a harmful monster,
The leaves, a huge family.

Jessica Martins (10)
St John Fisher RC Primary School, St Albans

Underneath The Tree

The tree is like a cave,
Loads of hands are creeping down.
Snakes are wriggling around,
The tree can't stop peering into your eyes.
Blossom is like snowflakes falling down,
It's a damp forest.
It's a white sheep floating in the air,
Underneath is a dungeon.

You walk out of the cave
And the place has changed.
The outside is colourful,
But the inside is dark.
The moss is like a limpet clinging on a tree,
It's wet and damp.

Catherine Nelson (10)
St John Fisher RC Primary School, St Albans

Life In A Field

The sparkly grass
Is like a tropical jungle,
I face a task to get out of the squelchy mud,
The mud is starting to crumble.

A worm slithering on top of the bendy grass
Is hunting for its prey,
Frightened, scared and alone,
Everywhere I turn there's something in my way.

An enormous hairy dandelion gets in my way,
Home is only a few thousand steps away.
A petal falls from the sky,
We're under attack in the tropical jungle.

Tom Anderson (10)
St John Fisher RC Primary School, St Albans

A Bird's Eye View

I feel like a pirate standing behind the wheel of my ship,
The leaves blow like a sail blowing in the spine-chilling wind.
The massive trunk like a mast,
Grass waving like a raging sea,
The rustling of leaves is thunder clapping
And clouds shaped like bolts of lightning.

Blossom falls and scatters in the wind like rain bouncing off rocks,
Ants surround my ship like sharks on their prey,
I feel like an eagle, watching scurrying animals across
the desert plain.
The bee is a cannonball flying like a bullet towards me,
I must protect my ship,
But risk my life I wouldn't do,
I leap like a frog from a lily pad.

My ship has been destroyed,
I swoop towards a pond, it is like a gleaming mirror.
A dragonfly is a dragon, red like blood,
I die on the spot like a raging storm,
When the sun breaks free from its grasp.

Oliver Fox (10)
St John Fisher RC Primary School, St Albans

The Giant Tree

My green leaves spreading over the sky,
Swaying and waving as the strong wind blows.
The falling leaves are birds swooping down,
With a wrinkly trunk growing bigger all the time,
In the spring I go from green to white,
I'm the biggest tree, day and night.

Joanna Robinson (10)
St John Fisher RC Primary School, St Albans

The Ant's Adventures

I looked up and saw grass like a never-ending rainforest,
Then a gust of wind came and a daisy crashed into me,
Then right up in the sky a big colourful thing came by,
The bench looked like the Millennium Stadium.
The tree was massive and looked like a giant monster.

Jack Ruane (10)
St John Fisher RC Primary School, St Albans

Under The Bench

The grass I'm in is as long as trees,
The grass is dancing all day long.
I can smell something beautiful,
I wonder what it is.
Piles of dead grass lies all around me,
A white cloud stands above me.
I turn around, a giant yellow plant stands above me.
I turn around again, but there is no white cloud.
Instead a giant monster is standing over me,
It's made of wood and is very tough.

Ryan Brown (10)
St John Fisher RC Primary School, St Albans

The Worm

W orm I am, I am a worm.
O n a tree I like to rest.
R ed is the colour of my body.
M olehill is where I live.

Mary Anne Pollitt (10)
St John Fisher RC Primary School, St Albans

The Scary Bedroom

I lie awake in my bed at night
And hope that nothing will give me a fright,
I hope I'll be asleep before the coming of the light.

There's a wardrobe in the corner of my room,
Then I see a shadow loom,
Am I resigned to my doom?

Is there a creature behind my bed?
Waiting to pounce upon my head,
If there is I'm surely dead.

I hear a noise beneath my bed,
Is it a monster with an ugly head?
Oh good, it's the cat, I'll cuddle her instead.

Lewis Colson (10)
St Joseph's In The Park Primary School, Hertingfordbury

I'd Rather . . .

I'd rather be big than slim,
I'd rather walk than swim,
I'd rather have a knee than a shin,
I'd rather smile than grin,
I'd rather have a mouth than a chin.

I'd rather have a brick than a stick,
I'd rather be slow than quick,
I'd rather give you a flick,
I'd rather be well than sick.

I'd rather have a tap that drips,
I'd rather be able to do flips,
I'd rather give in those slips,
I'd rather get some chips,
I'd rather have loads of ships.

Nicole Gerrick (10)
St Mary's CE Primary School, Rickmansworth

Mankind

Man's life is like a week. All weeks have beginnings and endings.
Being born on Monday, howling like the wolf of the night.
He is welcomed by smiling faces blocking out the light in
this new world.

Tuesday, he grows into the wailing, moaning beached whale.
When on land helpless to do anything,
Trying to stop himself from going to school.

Wednesday, he moves on into the next dreaded stage of life.
He is becoming the independent loner
Who knows how to survive living alone.

Thursday, he becomes the ruthless teenager trying to be
cool like everyone else.
Always on the move stopping every so often.

An adult, all mature and sentimental caring for behaviour, all posh.
Always knowing when to move. Staying or going.

On Saturday the OAPs take in so much knowledge they don't
have a clue what to do with it.
Either they keep it to themselves, or pass it down to their generation.

On Sunday in the jaws of death, he still bravely lives on.
Still enjoying the time he is in at the door of Death, D eath
swishes his scythe.
He dies but in honour. So much knowledge is lost forever.

Jack Finnan (9)
St Mary's CE Primary School, Rickmansworth

I'd Rather Be A . . .

I'd rather be a cat than a bird
I'd rather be first than third
I'd rather be a sentence than a word
I'd rather be a cool kid than a nerd.

Charlotte Rooke (10)
St Mary's CE Primary School, Rickmansworth

All This Land Is A Step

First, born as a foal, snuggling up to his mother in a cool,
comfortable sleep, a snoozing foal.
Second, a youngster brightening and waking up,
choosing to gallop around the field, bucking, daringly fighting.
Third, befriending the other horses,
learning how to run free, how to obey, how to fight back.
A saddle is placed, cold bit in the mouth, buckling to the
weight of a rider.
Fourth, prancing everywhere grandly, showing to all the world
how he can obey a rider on his back.
Fifth, leader of the herd, leading the others to safety,
teaching how to obey, run free, how to fight back.
His mother whinnies to him from the stable, her last mourning call.
Now he is on his own.
He slides down the pecking order.
He is now in the sixth stage and regarded old.
Young riders plod round on him. His sparkle is gone.
He has forgotten how to run, how to fight back.
In his seventh stage, he stumbles, falls,
closes his eyes and departs from this world,
ready to join his mother, who is galloping round in paradise.

Stephanie Frow (10)
St Mary's CE Primary School, Rickmansworth

Parents!

P arents think they're the boss
A nd they always get cross!
R ummaging and raging annoys them,
E verything bugs them!
N ever cleaning up my mess,
T op to bottom, they've ripped my dress!
S o parents are so annoying!

Laura FitzPatrick (9)
St Mary's CE Primary School, Rickmansworth

Keep On Smiling

It's hard to laugh when things go wrong,
It's easy to lose heart,
But if you can keep on smiling
It's certainly a start.
Happiness seems far away,
When days are long and sad,
But just as good times pass away,
So do all the bad.
Trouble always fades away,
If you can grin and bear it,
But call me if it gets too much
And I'll be there to share it.

Shelby Grayson (9)
St Mary's CE Primary School, Rickmansworth

Brothers

There are all sorts of brothers,
Big and small,
Short and tall,
There are brothers who are good,
There are brothers who are bad,
Some come happy, but some come sad,
Some share
And some don't care,
There is a caring one,
There is one who has no fun,
Some give you toys,
Some play with other boys,
But I like the brother who stays locked in
His room and doesn't bother,
Me!

Rosie Hammond (10)
St Mary's CE Primary School, Rickmansworth

I Saw A Strange World

I saw an ice cube give off sound
I saw a speaker melt in the sun
I saw a pen crack with clear fluid
I saw an egg spurt black ink
I saw a boy drink fresh blood
I saw a vampire play football in the hot sun
I saw a mouse woof and pant with a slobbery tongue
I saw a dog squeak with a high-pitched voice
I saw a skeleton jog non-stop for 7km
I saw a man sleep in a dusty coffin
I saw a tree watch TV at 11pm
I saw a kid grow branches
I saw a rich man drinking
I saw a drunk have a first class Cuban cigar.

Niall Brooks (10)
St Mary's CE Primary School, Rickmansworth

The Changing Seasons

Silver moons and silver shadows,
Golden suns and golden leaves,
Crimson colours, crimson sunsets.
A pure white night on Christmas Eve.

Crunchy snow thick and metallic,
Rustling leaves being touched and felt.
Blinding colours of evening sunsets,
The sun comes out and snow begins to melt.

The last of the snow,
The last of the sunshine,
The last of the vivid colours,
So what is next . . . ?

Rachel Hosking (10)
St Mary's CE Primary School, Rickmansworth

The Pyramid

The king of the desert,
Your stones rising high,
You almost appear
To be reaching the sky.

Golden sand all around you,
Bright sun overhead,
Inside your dark chasm
The pharaoh lies dead.

Egyptian king Ramesses,
The prince of the Nile,
I'll stay by your tomb
And linger awhile.

The people of Egypt
Raised you on high,
But now the ships of the desert
Just pass you by.

Your palace of splendour,
Your golden masked face,
Your wisdom, your riches,
Your passion and grace.

They built you a temple,
That adorns the fine sand,
A permanent reminder
Of one who once ruled the land.

From pharaoh to mummy,
Buried deep, deep below,
How they built your cathedral,
People still do not know.

So I'll stop and I'll wonder
And linger awhile
And pay my own tribute
To the prince of the Nile.

Chris Jones (9)
St Mary's CE Primary School, Rickmansworth

Read Me A Poem

Read me a poem
A poem a day
This is a poem
Made in May!

Read me a poem
About ghoulies and ghosts
While I sit by the fire
And eat my hot toast

Read me a poem
About a teddy bear
Which when Christmas came
His sweets he did share

You asked for a poem
A poem's right here
So stop playing music
And turn up your ears

Read me and read me
And read me again
Read me and read me
Right to the end

(Which is now!)

Olivia Jones (10)
St Mary's CE Primary School, Rickmansworth

Saul Sore

Saul saw his sore
He sawed his sore off
The sore got sorer than before
Saul's sore was really sore.

Matthew McLeod (8)
St Mary's CE Primary School, Rickmansworth

I Believe . . .

I believe there should be peace in the world,
In the north, south, east and west.
I believe that God made the world
And on the seventh day had a rest.

I believe that there should be no wars
In Iraq or Pakistan.
I believe that hunters shouldn't hunt animals,
Perhaps animals should do the same to man.

I believe that people should recycle rubbish,
To save the trees that stand.
I believe that humans shouldn't drop litter,
But use the bins on land.

I *used to* believe in fairytales
And act them out as plays,
But I'm a little older now
And see things in different ways.

Abigail Miles (10)
St Mary's CE Primary School, Rickmansworth

Anxious Ants

To us the grass is like a non-returning,
Deadly, terrifying forest which goes on forever.
The enormous giants block our light,
So our homes become cold and creepy,
Our bodies are like nests of small, crunchy bones,
To us a tree is like a skyscraper with evil,
Sharp, green claws which grab us,
When it's raining some of us get vital
And dangerous cuts, we feel as if Niagara Falls
Are collapsing on us,
We have to move swiftly through the world
Like a shark in the sea.

William Dent (10)
St Mary's CE Primary School, Rickmansworth

The Chewing Chocolate

Charlotte chewed a chocolate bar
Which had a cherry on the top
The chocolate chip bar was lovely
To chew with the cherry on the top
The chocolate bar was good to chew
During the church service all morning.

Charlotte Hindley (7)
St Mary's CE Primary School, Rickmansworth

The Boy From Applldy

There was a boy from Applldy
Who went to see a shark,
On the way he met a dog
Who gave a very loud bark.

The boy went screaming,
Running into town,
Then he hit a tree
And the apples fell down.

The farmer got mad and hit the boy
And told him to give away money,
Finally the farmer let him go
And the boy was crying for his mummy.

The boy was crying
Until he reached home,
Then he gasped to see a surprise
Because his mum was covered with foam.

His mum explained
Why she was covered in foam,
She was crazily attacked
Behind the Millennium Dome!

Thomas Mitchell (9)
St Mary's CE Primary School, Rickmansworth

The Cute Little Fish

Kara the cat ate colourful fish
With cute little spots all over their fins
Another cat came and cuddled her
And said
'Can I have a colourful fish
With cute little spots all over its fins?'
Kara the cat said, 'You can get it yourself!'

Kara Glynn (8)
St Mary's CE Primary School, Rickmansworth

Peacock, Peacock

Peacock, peacock
Look at your beautiful, dazzling feathers on your tail,
Lots of swirls and patterns like eyes,
The way the feathers spread out wide and ripple in the wind.

Ant, ant
How come you're so strong?
You are such a minute animal,
Yet you can lift bread onto your back
And carry it about.

Swan, swan
With your neck so long
And your bright orange beak,
You can spread your strong, spotless white wings
And swoop away into the distance.

Snake, snake
Slithering slowly along,
With your tongue flickering endlessly,
Your venomous fangs glinting in the sun.

Daisy Norman (9)
St Mary's CE Primary School, Rickmansworth

A Hint Of Promise

A proud mother watching over her beautiful newborn,
First breath of life, first taste of sweet emerald grass,
Bucking, nipping and playing with his joyful friends,
Galloping, running free, wind in his coat, herd in front,
Proud father leading the herd, his soft chestnut and gold coat
And his silky white and silver mane and tail,
Cocky colt he is fighting other stallions, protecting mares,
He is now herd leader, proud, bold and strong,
Wild pony, wild stamina like a rock,
Never standing down to a fight, now he is proud,
Watching his son prancing around the herd,
Bold and big, nothing stopping him like his father,
Free spirit!

Victoria Sexton (10)
St Mary's CE Primary School, Rickmansworth

The Little Squirrel

There once was a little squirrel,
Who sat on a ledge,
A cat tried to pounce on him,
But fell in the hedge.
The little squirrel almost fell,
Then up above him he smelt a lovely smell,
'Roasted acorns,'
Were the words his mother did cry,
So he jumped off the ledge with a watchful eye,
The cat was gone so he climbed the tree,
For he was ready for a hearty tea.

Megan Danskine (10)
St Mary's CE Primary School, Rickmansworth

Calum Likes Chocolate Chip Cookies

Calum likes chocolate chip cookies and cherry cake
And Coca-Cola
Calum likes cricket and chocolate ice cream
Calum likes kicking balls.

Calum Joyce (7)
St Mary's CE Primary School, Rickmansworth

Guess Who?

Four little black eyes looking at me,
Eight little feet clean as can be,
Two little pink noses sniffing away
And two little bottoms sticking out of the hay.

Two big carrots disappearing bit by bit,
Two bowls of food that get eaten very quick,
One water bottle that drips all day,
Two noisy toys with which they play.

Out in the long grass playing in their run,
Lying on their fat sides and sitting in the sun,
Squeaking whenever I come near,
Chatting to each other when the coast is clear.

Two little black eyes looking for trouble,
Brown and white and black, it must be Bubble,
Two more black eyes having a peek,
Smooth and brown and shiny, it must be Squeak.

They live in my bedroom at the end of my bed,
In a cage full of sawdust they wait to be fed.
They run into their igloos playing hide-and-seek,
These are my guinea pigs, Bubble and Squeak.

Hannah Deamer (10)
St Mary's CE Primary School, Rickmansworth

My Magic Locket

(Inspired by Kit Wright)

I will put in my locket . . .

The first glance of a newborn foal,
The first light of the world,
The last breath of a dying person,
The last sound of a creature.

I will put in my locket . . .

A hair of a beast, extinct long ago,
The cry of this world when the sun gets too close,
A mist undefeated and gloating in triumph.

I will put in my locket . . .

The memories on my shelves both bad and good,
The trickle of a cool white stream,
The smell of warm, soaked hay.

I will put in my locket . . .

The scale of the dragon King Arthur killed,
The feel of the clouds freshly risen,
The sound of a pony's hooves fresh on the ground.

My locket is fashioned out of . . .

Gold melted by dwarves skilled and brisk,
The stars I caught last night, and the moon,
A voice of a genie unlocks the latch.

I will wear my locket . . .

When I lie on the coral,
When I gallop over the sky,
When I sleep on the sun.

Emma Cookson (10)
St Mary's CE Primary School, Rickmansworth

Night

Spiders shall come out tonight
I'm sure you will get a fright
Spiders shall crawl over your family's
Bodies, yours shall be first

Don't worry

The zombies will lay their eggs
Thousands all in your hair
Don't worry they will disappear
In 1000 years

Don't worry

Mum and Dad won't be there
When you are screaming in scare
Zombies and spiders are nothing
Compared to big soul eating bear

Don't worry

The big soul-eating bear
Shall take your soul
Like a big black hole
I'd watch out if I were you!

Don't worry
Have a nice night!

Lily Kemp (8)
St Mary's CE Primary School, Rickmansworth

Christmas Poem

It's Christmas and I'm having fun
The party of love has just begun
Celebrations and parties
Are wriggling in my tum.

Grace Russell (8)
St Mary's CE Primary School, Rickmansworth

In My Garden

In my garden I can see
Flowers, trees and buzzing bees,
I can see the luscious green grass
And models made out of brass,
I see little creatures running up my legs,
My mum hanging up the washing on the pegs,
Balls being thrown high up in the air,
The people throwing them just don't care,
All the things I love in my garden.

I can smell the flowers sweet,
Oh it is a treat,
I smell the river flowing by
And the grass which is really dry,
The blossom on the trees,
The pollen which is collected by the bees,
All the things I love in my garden.

I can hear the water passing by
And someone in a deep cry,
A cat purring and moaning,
An old man groaning,
The wind blowing strongly,
Someone being shouted at for doing something wrongly,
All the things in my garden I love.

I enjoy my garden the most,
I don't really want to boast,
Playing games in my garden,
Not waiting for the ground to harden,
In the summer, winter, autumn and spring,
Not one day goes by when I'm not happy in my garden.

Jessica Charman (9)
St Mary's CE Primary School, Rickmansworth

The History Of Hanover House

George I
When old Anne had died;
Along came George with his pride.
He didn't speak English,
So his servants couldn't finish
The castle before he died!

George II
Along came a guy called . . . George
His blacksmiths worked in a forge,
He always was eating,
Never liked competing -
And 'never' fell into a gorge.

George III
George III was great!
But never used a rake
He went very crazy . . .
And extravagantly lazy,
Everyone believed him to be fake.

George IV
George IV had a grumpy mood
Gorging down his food.
Piggy as a pig;
Didn't want a wig,
No one called him *dude.*

Alexander Horrox-White (8)
St Mary's CE Primary School, Rickmansworth

Winter Beach

The icy spray blows off the sea,
Breakwaters stick up like giant fingers,
Breakers white and frothy like cotton wool streaks,
Sandy needle pricks sting my face,
As pebbles collide they go clickety-clack,
The beach is deserted, I'm the only one here.

Sarah Pearce (11)
St Mary's CE Primary School, Rickmansworth

My Dog Rosie

My dog Rosie is very clever,
My dog Rosie runs around forever.
My dog Rosie is the best,
My dog Rosie likes to have a rest.

My dog Rosie has a black tail.
My dog Rosie collects the mail.
My dog Rosie wears a red collar.
My dog Rosie hates it when I holler.

My dog Rosie is very black.
My dog Rosie chases me round a track.
My dog Rosie eats bugs.
My dog Rosie plays with slugs.

My dog Rosie is very friendly.
My dog Rosie is quite bendy.
My dog Rosie likes the colour yellow.
My dog Rosie likes to eat a marshmallow.

Amy Bullen (10)
St Mary's CE Primary School, Rickmansworth

Stars

The stars shine brightly
In the early night breeze
The light glistens on the ground
And reflects on my knees

I see the stars before me
In the night sky
They glow brightly in my face
And I just wonder why

The day is just beginning
All the stars go away
Just for one more night
And come back the next day!

Elena Turner (11)
St Mary's CE Primary School, Rickmansworth

Harry Potter And The Prisoner Of Azkaban

Far inside the shrieking shack
Lying in wait is Sirius Black
Ron is dragged down below
Underneath the whomping willow
Harry and Hermione go after him
Next follows Professor Lupin
Black and Lupin tell their tale
All about Wormtail's horrible betrayal.

Sarah Blacklock (11)
St Mary's CE Primary School, Rickmansworth

The Things That Used To Spook Me

There are lots of things that used to spook me
Just small things like a bumblebee
But some of them are big things
Like these small creatures with little black wings
They turn into vampires you see
And I hate it when they bite me
There are also the witches
They are full of trickses
Casting lots of spells
Turning people into wells
Then there is Frankenstein
He's no fun, he always whines
There are also lots and lots of ghosts
They throw at me, hot buttered toast
Sometimes I'm scared of bad dreams
I dream I'm drowning in a stream
I'm scared of spiders scuttling around
When they're spinning their webs going round and round
But I'm not scared now I'm OK
I'll tell you more another day.

Anya Wronski (9)
St Mary's CE Primary School, Rickmansworth

Morning

The bright sun shining through my window
Morning
Birds flying in the sky
Morning
The TV chattering
Morning
The smell of bacon sizzling in the pan
Morning
The kettle boiling
Morning
The smell of burnt toast in the air
Morning
The tea is steaming hot
Morning
It's time to go to school
Morning.

Apple Paz (9)
St Mary's CE Primary School, Rickmansworth

My Football Team

A rsenal are the best
R ather better than the rest
S coring goals as they come
E arning points as no other team has done
N o other team can compare
A rsenal play very, very fair
L ehmann is number one, as he has played as he should have done.

Oliver Blake (9)
St Mary's CE Primary School, Rickmansworth

The Garden

When bluebells are ringing
And the river is flowing
When the birds are singing
And taking a bath
Kids are playing
And jumping around
The dogs are barking
And sniffing the ground.

Lucy Harrison (8)
St Mary's CE Primary School, Rickmansworth

The Knight

The knight who wept forever long
His one true love sang a song
To say goodbye forever
Now she lives in total harmony
And sits back in the very chair on the
Very balcony that she said goodbye
For the last time.

Rhys Evans (10)
St Mary's CE Primary School, Rickmansworth

The Best Team In All The Land

Whose home kit is red and white? *Arsenal.*
Who won the Premiership title? *Arsenal* did.
Whose nifty footwork scored nearly all the goals?
The best player in all the land, Thierry Henry of course.
Robert Pires and Jose Reyas did their best so did all the rest.
Arsenal went the season without being beaten,
The first since Preston North End,
Not bad I suppose for a great team like *Arsenal.*

Richard Watt (9)
St Mary's CE Primary School, Rickmansworth

My Family

My sister, she loves performing,
she does dance, gym and flute.
She always makes up dances
and helps me with all the moves.

My mum, she was a sports woman
but now she teaches sport.
She cooks and cleans and shops for us
and I thank her very much.

My dad he loves his fishing,
he catches carp and pike.
He waters all the flowers
and I help him every week.

As I am the youngest
I ride my bike a lot.
I have a purple bedroom
and I love my family lots!

Rebecca Miles (7)
St Mary's CE Primary School, Rickmansworth

My Cat

My cat is white
But he gives everyone a fright
He has green eyes
But fat thighs
He can run
And have fun
He gets in a mood
Without his food
And that is why I love him!

Amber Clark (8)
St Mary's CE Primary School, Rickmansworth

Morning Time

When I wake up in the morning
all I do is keep on yawning

I get up and put on my dress
and get in a very big mess

I untangle myself
and get a book from the shelf

The book is called 'The Dare Game'
it's a very unusual book name

I go into the bathroom and brush my teeth
and look into the garden down beneath

I walk into the garden to look at the flowers
and look up at the trees that are as tall as towers

And that's what happens at morning time.

Abigail Clarke (9)
St Mary's CE Primary School, Rickmansworth

A Great Day

I went to the funfair
And went on a swinging chair
I won loads of prizes
Of all different sizes
I watched a band
And they were grand
It was so much fun
Playing in the sun
We went to the farm
And there was a horse in the barn.

Jessica Bellamy (8)
St Mary's CE Primary School, Rickmansworth

Munching, Munchy Monsters

Munching, Munchy monsters
Munching Munchies
Munching Munchies munched munchy monsters
Munching Munchies made munching monsters
Have monster-munching pox
Then munching monsters ran after the munching Munchies
Then the munching Munchies landed in Minorca.

Oliver Mitchell (8)
St Mary's CE Primary School, Rickmansworth

Grumpy Gareth

Gareth grumbled with a gorilla
as it ate its grapefruit

The gorilla gracefully gave
Gareth a green grapefruit

The grapefruit made Gareth
grumble more.

Gareth Jones (8)
St Mary's CE Primary School, Rickmansworth

My PlayStation

My PlayStation lives in the loft
The games I play are hard, not soft
The buttons I press are quite sticky
The games to win are very tricky
One day I will be a professional player
On my PlayStation I will blow up the mayor
I will soon take over the world on my PlayStation.

Luke Hammond (8)
St Mary's CE Primary School, Rickmansworth

Butterfly

B rightly coloured wings stand as powerful as the sun shines,
U nbelievable and delicate body,
T remendous beauty sparkles our eyes,
T he touch of a butterfly makes us laugh,
E ach early step it takes shows the goldness it has,
R aspberry smell makes you feel warm and cosy,
F loating air follows it through soundly and invisibly,
L ively but small, what effort it puts,
Y oung or adult it certainly brightens the day.

Bhavika Tanna (10)
St Mary's CE Primary School, Rickmansworth

School Dinners

What is this goo
Upon my plate?
It looks as if it's sat there
Since quarter past eight.

Rock-hard pizza
And manky chips,
Don't make me eat it
It'll stick to my lips!

Icky custard
Comes in lumps,
If I don't eat it
The dinner lady grumps.

Down it goes
Into my tummy,
A disgusting child
Would say, 'It's yummy!'

Andrew Leddington (9)
St Mary's CE Primary School, Rickmansworth

My Magic Box

(Based on 'Magic Box' by Kit Wright)

I will put in my box . . .

The sound of a hummingbird whistling in the trees,
The grey clouds and their silver linings,
The autumn colours falling from the trees.

I will put in my box . . .

A golden feather from a golden eagle,
A purple petal from a pink pansy,
A piece of fur from a tabby cat.

I will put in my box . . .

The smell of a special sunflower swaying in the wind,
A claw from a scary scorpion,
The sound of the cold winter snow falling.

The box is made from . . .

The sides of the box are woven petals from a hundred roses,
They have been sewn together with spiders' silk
And among the hundred roses are a thousand diamonds.

The box is made from . . .

The hinges are from golden ladybird shells,
The only key is from one hair of a lion's mane,
I will treasure my magic box forever.

Heather Tysoe (9)
St Mary's CE Primary School, Rickmansworth

Luke The Lollipop

Luke looked like a lucky lollipop
And Luke liked licking lollipops
So Luke licked himself
And it lasted as long as a lemon
Luke liked looking like a lollipop
So Luke will always look like a lollipop.

Luke Mitchell (8)
St Mary's CE Primary School, Rickmansworth

Morning Time

The birds singing gently and beautifully
The noise of rattling lorries, the sound
Of your dad snoring.
What time is it?

Mark Lineton (9)
St Mary's CE Primary School, Rickmansworth

Ghost

Evil moon,
In dead blue sky,
Mist suffocates ground
And to naked eye,
A faded figure,
Sad and wry.

And if that person
Followed the cursed male,
Denied of life so young,
By means of betrayal,
Of a joke gone horribly wrong,
Here's how his life did fail.

Down by the water's edge,
Where the current is so strong,
He was left to slide into the lake,
By friends that did him wrong,
They did not come to rescue or aid in any way,
Their friend as he slipped far and long.

And so the small child,
Met his dreadful fear,
Of drowning in a harsh cold lake
And can just disappear
And as for his unsung song,
It is so shrill no one can hear . . .

Stuart Found (11)
St Mary's CE Primary School, Rickmansworth

Oh Brother

My little brother is always annoying me,
He follows me around like a big bumblebee,
He takes my toys,
He makes plenty of noise,
Messing up my room,
In a great big *boom!*
He always wants to tag along,
He asks me questions then says I'm wrong!
He seems to like telling tales,
But when he's told off he wails and wails.
When it's his bedtime I'm so glad,
It's one way to stop him from being bad,
Little brothers are a pain you see,
But I'll always love him and he'll always love me.

George Furr (9)
St Mary's CE Primary School, Rickmansworth

My Mum And Dad

My mum and dad are so nice
If there is a cool book that I like they buy it for me
If I want to watch TV or go on my PS2 they let me
Except when it's swimming
When I have done something that I have not done before
They really congratulate me
They even give me sweets
My mum and dad are so cool
You should have a mum and dad like mine.

Lucy White (9)
St Mary's CE Primary School, Rickmansworth

Through The Window - A Visual Rap

I look out the window and what do I see?
The boring old window staring back plainly.

I look out the window and what do I see?
A twisting, buzzing bumblebee.

I look out the window and what do I see?
The lifeless body of a lifeless tree.

I look out the window and what do I see?
My sister's best friend, the amazing Lee.

I look out the window and what do I see?
My mum saying, 'It's time for tea.'

I look out the window and what do I see?
The superstitious smile of a chimpanzee.

I look out the window and what do I see?
An awesome alien blaring, 'Blee, blee, blee'.

I look out the window and what do I see?
I forgot it's a mirror and look, there's me!

Bryn Lansdown (9)
St Mary's CE Primary School, Rickmansworth

My Best Friend, Frank

My best friend is four inches tall,
He doesn't say a word at all.
I love to watch him bustle and scurry,
Very busy and in a great hurry.
But most of the time he's curled in a heap,
Ears flat on his head and fast asleep.

He lives in my room in a bright red cage,
He is timid, gentle and never in a rage.
He always listens if I'm upset,
Much more than just your average pet.
My best friend has eyes that shine,
He is a hamster and he is all mine.

Henry Frakes (8)
St Mary's CE Primary School, Rickmansworth

This Cat

This cat will do anything
She'll run around at night
She'll creep along the rooftops
And sleep through daylight

This cat will do anything
She'll dance to pop videos if she likes
But when we go to a posh beach
She'll try and catch a motorbike

This cat will do anything
She'll try and wear my tops
She'll cuddle up my teddy bear
And drink my soda pops

This cat will do anything
Her fur is soft and fine
Her nose tickles as she sniffs
But best of all . . . *she's mine!*

Gemma Fenlon (11)
St Mary's CE Primary School, Rickmansworth

The Gunners

My idols,
The Gunners,
Always fast,
Always loving every task,
Happy days,
Sad days,
When David Seamen left the team,
A season unbeaten,
The Gunners are the best,
Better than the rest!

Rebekah McNamara (11)
St Paul's RC Primary & Nursery School, Cheshunt

Mr Volcano

I can explode and destroy with a bang and a boom,
So get in your car and go vroom vroom vroom!

Don't come near me; don't even come close,
Because I'm sure you'll regret it, you and me both!

I can sweat with fiery fury when I am cross,
So step away now or I'll show you who's boss!

I can burn anything in my sight
With my destructive, fiery, flaming might!

Don't even try to get in my way
Or you will burn and you will pay!

Robert Kuzik (11)
St Paul's RC Primary & Nursery School, Cheshunt

Sunlight

Glowing brightly peeps the sun,
Here to sparkle all day long,
She waves her arms and kindly shouts,
'Don't you love it when the sun comes out?'
Her grand and glossy coat of joy,
Towers over girls and boys,
Her golden glow is here to stay
And wipes cloudiness and rain away,
Golden houses, golden town,
Sparkle in the sun,
Glittering, twinkling, dazzling blaze
And people having fun!

Katie Erin Evans (10)
St Paul's RC Primary & Nursery School, Cheshunt

The Jungle

I walked through the jungle,
scared as can be.
As I walked on,
something hit my knee.

I carried on walking through the jungle,
until I saw a key.
Then I saw a door and pushed it in
and then I was free.

Then I was in another jungle,
where I saw a tree.
There was a monkey up the top,
who was juggling with a pea.

I walked on through the jungle,
when somebody asked me for tea.
Then they gave me soup,
but in it was a bee.

I walked on through the jungle,
then I saw a flea.
I quickly ran away,
before it said anything to me.

Ryan Barrett (10)
St Paul's RC Primary & Nursery School, Cheshunt

Love

Love is red
Love smells lovely
Love tastes like cherries and cream
Love is sweet
Love is beautiful
Love feels calm
Love is bright red like a rose.

Kelly Brooks (9)
St Paul's RC Primary & Nursery School, Cheshunt

Tiger

Creeping through the rainforest
Crouching low
A tiger crouches
Ready to pounce on
The young antelope

The antelope flees away
The tiger
Pounces
Missed the antelope
Gets up again
And pounces!

Antelope for tea tonight!

How nice.

Chloe Geaves (11)
Sandon JMI School

The Cloadews

Deep underground in the Earth's crust
Live a race that are called the Cloadews
These raging, ripping, ravenous beasts feast upon the meat of Noles
They always sleep in the morning, they never sleep at night
All they do is eat nature's delights
The Cloadews are a fearless race who never walk away from a fight
But I have a Cloadew of my own and he is quite alright!

Edward Shaw (11)
Sandon JMI School

Danger

In the darkness of the forest a child hides
Hungry it searches for food
It hears a rustle
In a flash he was gone

In the darkness of the forest
No children can you see
In their place a pile of bones lay . . .

Julia Scheepers (10)
Sandon JMI School

The Creature

Huge, fearsome, vicious and violent,
Wild, scary, hugely hairy,
Paws as big as paws can be,
Chestnut colour,
Who am I?

Lion.

Julia Alderman (10)
Sandon JMI School

Who Am I?

No one comes here anymore,
In this gloomy forest,
I'm hairy with not many feathers on my wings,
I come out at night, *woo,* who am I?

Harriet Crouch (11)
Sandon JMI School

The Mungel Wungel Tree

In a deep and dark jungle,
Lives a weird and wonderful Mungel.
This marvellous tree
Fabulous to be
Is the Mungel Wungel tree.

The leaves are long and curly,
They whisper very early,
'Look out! The bird
Is about,' they shout
On the Mungel Wungel tree.

All the branches are short and stumpy
Ugly knots are big, hairy and lumpy,
But the trunk is so big,
It looks like a twig,
On the Mungel Wungel tree.

But one sunny day in the night,
The Mungel Wungel tree got a fright,
A man called Max
With a huge axe
Cut the Mungel Wungel tree.

Ed Potts (11)
Sandon JMI School

Buried Treasure

Beyond, in the wondrous world,
The armies are looking for their lost gold.
Buried by ancestors,
Forgotten it was there.
Lost treasure,
Day by day,
Night by night,
Finding and digging,
Forever.

Michael Watson (10)
Sandon JMI School

Frdog

Deep in the big swamp,
The big and slimy Frdog,
Lives in a big hole.

It goes *cwoof!* when it's
Trying to get its prey
And hides in its hideout.

Frdog lives in a slimy place
In the middle
Of the slimy swamp.

It jumps onto its prey
And then it chews it up
And then leaves the bones.

Joeanne Chandler (10)
Sandon JMI School

Who Am I?

Long slithering,
Slimy slider,
Tiggly tongue,
Human snapper,
Tight squeezer,
Thin jumper,
Who am I?
A snake.

Thomas Bradbury (10)
Sandon JMI School

The Spinner

There it was
Long and nasty
Eight legs creeping towards me
Each are hairy and horrible
As long as nothing
But as thick as could be
Horrible it was

Named the Spinner
Winding a web
Staring up at me
With all its legs ready to pounce
I ran and ran.

Francesca Gascoine (10)
Sandon JMI School

Brothers

Brothers are horrible
Brothers call you names
Brothers go on about things
They play on silly computer games

Brothers nick your money
Brothers beat you up
Brothers turn music on
And tell your nasty stuff

But my brother is not like that
My brother is totally different
My brother is not that bad
But he does make me feel glad.

Ashleigh Pinchen (11)
Sauncey Wood Primary School

Senseless

Loud clattering, rattling, people shouting,
It sounds like a foreign language to me,
Some crying, some laughing lost in the sea of emotions,
Then a prick searing through,
The prick of a needle feels like someone stabbing my heart,
Touch of a friendly nurse trying to comfort me, heal me after my loss,
Then the smooth curve of the spoon,
The taste of sugary medicine sliding like grit down my throat,
Then something else, something warm, hot, spicy . . .
But it's not nice, it's horrid,
Horrid hospital curry trying to creep down into the pit of my stomach,
The sight sad, some laughing,
Though some are crying as the wall leers at others' misfortune,
People hurt inside and out,
As she comes closer I can smell her perfume nearing closer too,
Now the smell that everyone hates,
The smell of death mingling with disinfectant,
Nearing me closer, closer, closer . . .

Georgia Wilding (11)
Sauncey Wood Primary School

My Confusing Nightmare

N asty gargoyles scaring my mates,
I nfant spirits racing through the sky,
G raveyards with the zombies of fate,
H ot fires flaming nearer and nearer,
T errible ghosts going to the fair,
M onsters worse than in Scooby-Doo!
A ll the scarers ruining your hair,
R ebels taunting people in the street,
E veryone gets 'em, it's a *nightmare!*

Deepavna Thankey (11)
Sauncey Wood Primary School

Writing This Poetry

I heard a thing,
The topic is bad,
A nightmare,
Hard,
It makes me so sad.

Try to let this change,
It wouldn't change,
Stays the same,
It's crazy, insane,
I hate the pain.

Try to beat the tears,
Stop crying!
Stop lying!
Try to stop the fears,
Maybe feels like dying?

I'm hoping,
Hoping against hope,
Screaming,
Fighting,
For some changes,
Slowly slipping away,
Yeah, so is hope,
Some changes yet?
Nope!

I feel so cowardly,
Terribly cowardly,
Because all this drama
Is just because
I have to write this poetry.

Gwen Jing (11)
Sauncey Wood Primary School

The Street

Drumming, banging and keyboard
Playing can only mean one thing.
It's the street dog band!
They're riding their motorbikes
Wearing dark glasses and studded collars
They're stealing from the butcher's
Making music as they go
Soon they'll be in concert
Singing their latest song
Guitars, drum kits, a keyboard
Are all part of the street dog band
The dogs are always on the streets
So if you go out, watch out for the street dog band.

Mollie Milnthorpe (9)
Sauncey Wood Primary School

In The Rainforest

I stand in a soggy, wet and sticky place,
Around me the air is humid and misty,
Howler monkeys scamper in the top of the trees,
I hear howls and echoes,
Down on the ground there is mud,
Here insects sleep,
Very noisy, chirrup, chirrup, chirrup,
Buzzzz and whirr,
Everything listens and watches,
Slithery, stern, salmon-pink snake,
Wiggly, wicked, wandering wild pig,
Pink, purple, pretty parrots,
Jumping, jumbo, jungle jaguar,
Everything listens and watches
In the rainforest.

Ella Wright (7)
Wheatcroft School

In The Rainforest

I stand in a rainforest, around me the air is damp and misty,
Howler monkey in the sky singing and echoing,
Around my feet insects rustle and chirp
Everything watches and listens,
Smooth, stripy, shiny snake,
A wiggly wily wicked wild pig
A playful perfect pink parrot,
A jazzy jumping jungle jaguar,
In the rainforest.

Paige Farnham (7)
Wheatcroft School

In The Rainforest

I stand in yucky wet mud in every shade of green
Around me the air is damp, wet and humid
Howler monkeys high above me in the tree tops I hear echoes, howls and shrieks
Round my feet in the bushes, on the ground,
The sound of insects flying round and round,
Chirps, high-pitched droning and buzz, buzz, buzzing.
Sparkling, shiny, stern snake,
Whiskery, wise and wiggly wild pig,
Plotting, pretty, playful parrots,
Jolly, jazzy, jumpy jaguar.

Katy Anker (7)
Wheatcroft School

Dolphin

As soft as the grass,
As small as a gate,
Their voices like the sea,
As blue as the waves,
As deep as the sky.

Elinor Clarkson (9)
Wheatcroft School

A Polar Bear!

The polar bear's bright topaz eyes are searching for food far off,
Her mouth waters when she notices a seal slide into the sea,
She's listening,
Listening hard with her dazzling white ears,
Her sniff so quiet that even an elephant couldn't hear it,
Her fur swaying in the breeze,
Feet padding through the snow,
Watching her prey.

Zoe Evans (8)
Wheatcroft School

Animal Poem

A long nose, shiny and black sniffing around the grass,
Eight claws, sharp and black scratching along the fence,
Feet stamping along, silver and grey in the sunlight,
Stretchy legs, long and grey, walking in the park,
The wavy, curved tail waving around in the wind,
Pointy ears triangle-shaped, hearing everything,
Some glittery, black, shiny eyes, you can see in the dark,
A barking, round head as cute as can be,
A large, grey body moving forward,
Fluffy, straight fur flicking all around.

Kathryn Auguste (8)
Wheatcroft School

The Baby Lamb

The fur was pearl-white and it was blowing in the wind,
The head was nodding about, the head was pearl-white,
The feet were dark black and they were trotting along,
The ears were listening and they were pearl, pearl-white,
She had teeth a bit yellow and she was eating grass.

Molly Wakeling (8)
Wheatcroft School

Goldie's Funeral

Bury her deep, down deep, safe in the earth's cold keep,
Bury her deep.

No more blowing bubbles,
No more mouthing troubles,
No more cleaning out,
No more swimming about,
No more eating food.

Bury her deep, down deep,
She is beyond warm sleep,
She will not wake in the morning,
She will not see the dawning,
Bury her deep.

Sarah Robertson (9)
Wheatcroft School

Tiger! Tiger!

Tiger, tiger in the tree,
All he's doing is staring with glee.
Watching a hare running past,
Running quickly, running fast.

Tiger, tiger ready to pounce,
Tiger, tiger ready to bounce,
Tiger, tiger looking tough,
Tiger, tiger playing rough.

Tiger, tiger ripping apart,
Tiger, tiger tearing his heart,
Tiger, tiger eating his flesh,
Tiger, tiger looking at the mess.

Tiger, tiger in the night,
Watching the moon with its glinting light,
All of the animals with terrible fright,
Because of the tiger ready to fight.

James Rogers (9)
Wheatcroft School

My Puppy

I have a puppy who is
Cuddly and cute
She likes it when my sister plays
The flute

My puppy runs about
At night
She likes it when I turn
On the light

My puppy likes to eat
Her food
When she is in a
Good mood

My puppy likes to go for
A walk
When I tell my sister
Not to talk.

Louise Curtis (9)
Wheatcroft School

Dangerous Dinosaur

The dinosaur has a hard bite
The dinosaur is a killer

The dinosaur shakes the ground
The dinosaur has sharp claws

The dinosaur has red eyes
The dinosaur has sharp teeth

The dinosaur has a swishing tail
The dinosaur scratches his prey.

Samuel Brown (7)
Wheatcroft School

I Like The Sea

I like swimming in the sea
I see loads of fishes and they see me

The octopus are orange
The jellyfish are pink
The water smells nice
But the shark's breath stinks

I wish there were dolphins
'Cause I think they're cool
There's some now, they're going to school
With their cute, sweet smile and their shiny golden skin
And behind them flapping is their beautiful fin

I see some mermaids playing with jewels
They chuck out all the bright ones, they must be fools.
I feel so happy now and I just want to shout out loud,
I love the sea and I think it rules!

Damini Kotecha (10)
Wheatcroft School

Enormous Dinosaur

A dinosaur is very loud
A dinosaur is very proud

A dinosaur is very teary
A dinosaur is very scary

A dinosaur is a big cheat
A dinosaur has big feet

A dinosaur is very loud
A dinosaur is very proud.

Bethany Fitzsimmons (7)
Wheatcroft School

My Toy Dinosaur

Good smeller
Always a teller

Enormous bite
Hunts more at night

Gets a pail
With his tail

Swishing head
His name is Ted.

Sarah Nichol (7)
Wheatcroft School

Rubbish

Old jars
Toy buses
Dusty doors
Holey shoes
Sewer rats
Old bones
Old tyres
Dirty biros
Dirty brushes
Old floors
Dirty loos
Dirty bats
Dirty combs
Coil of wire
Rubbish!

Michael Gillmor (9)
Widford School

Rubbish

Coke cans, rubber bands
Banana peel, great deal
Pencil sharpenings, loads of markings
Burnt toast, chicken roast
Old rags, paper bags
Old T-shirt, Pepsi that makes you burp
Rotten ham, chicken, lamb
Popped balloons, broken spoons
Rotten fish, broken dish
Bent forks, roasted pork
Broken buckets, chicken nuggets
Flat tyre, greasy wire
Apple core, more and more!

Tom Hollylee (9)
Widford School

Rubbish

Half-chewed shoes, seats from loos,
Toy cars, smashed jars,
Punctured balls, bent tools,
Old tyres, hair dryers,
Paint pot, smashed cot,
Baby toys, Game Boys,
Coat hangers, chips and bangers,
All the rubbish you throw out
Is a very big amount.

Patrick Findlay (9)
Widford School

The Magician's Cupboard

Cloaks and hats, big black cats,
Wands and stars, books and jars,
Magic spells fill the air, lots of rubbish everywhere,
Spiders turning into rats, dark and gloomy big brown bats,
Rabbits jumping into hats, hooting owls that stand on racks,
Frogs are jumping everywhere, brown ones, green ones,
watch them stare,
Lotions, potions everywhere, broomsticks, cauldrons,
Please beware!

Caitlin Mellors (9)
Widford School

A Magician's Cupboard

Four dead mice, packet of rice
Purple flour, Eiffel Tower
Eyeballs, monster's call
Spell book, pirate's hook
Golden drawers, dragon's claws
Troll's drool, velvet stool
Black cat, witch's hat
Magic wand, frogspawn pond
Empty jar, plastic car
50 ants, magician's pants
Silver chain, thunder and rain
All these things
In a magician's cupboard.

Abigail Prowse (8)
Widford School

The Magician's Cupboard

Dusty books, cloaks on hooks
Magic wands, frogs in ponds
Snapped broomsticks, several toothpicks!
Purple potions, white lotions
Smelly garlic fills the air
Rabbits jumping everywhere!
Flying bats and starry hats
Owls that hoot, big black boots
Please don't go there!

Anna Lowry (9)
Widford School

The Magician's Cupboard

Dragon's liver, golden river
Snake's skin, a fish's fin,
Monster's eyeballs, parrot's call
Spell book, Captain Hook
Troll's drool, builder's tools
Black bat, wings that flap
Bouncing frog, warthog
Jar of blood, coffee mug
90 ants, magician's pants
A big golden shield, poppy fields
All these things
In a magician's cupboard!

Hannah McGill (8)
Widford School

The Magician's Cupboard

Dusty book, coats on hooks,
Sour potions, dirty lotions,
Old wands, dirty bonds,
Wicked spell books, rusty door hooks,
Pointed hats, black cats,
Dark and gloomy, big hat loony,
Doors creaking, paws reaching.

Jordan Iliffe (9)
Widford School

The Things We Eat

Flour powder, lemon sour
Fudge cake, milkshake
Roast lamb, sandwich ham
Boiled egg, nutmeg
Orange juice, chocolate mousse
Black coffee, chewy toffee
All the things we forgot to eat
Now it smells like stinky feet.

Helena Page (9)
Widford School

The Magician's Cupboard

Rats and cats
Big scary bats
Lotion for a motion
Ready for the ocean
He has notion
To sail the ocean
Scary legs
Big fat heads
Brown soup, ready when it whoops.

Joseph Wiggin (8)
Widford School

My Room

Books, toys,
Paper, pens,
Pencils, drawings,
Bags, colouring pencils,
Game Boys, board games,
Toy guns, dummies,
TV, DVD,
DVD remote, TV remote,
Video remote, toy cars, joke books,
All these things put up,
Dumped on the floor or dumped on the bed,
That's what my room looks like.

Tristan Brownhill (8)
Widford School

My Room

My big bed with my teds,
My ted's fluffy, my bed's puffy,
My bed's comfy, my bed's lovely
And my teddies like it too.
Stars and lights on the ceiling,
Gives me such a nice warm feeling,
When I'm lying on my bed,
Cuddling my big fat ted.

Shannon Woodley (9)
Widford School

Rubbish

Banana skins in the bins,
Apple core, that's a bore,
Plastic bags full of mags,
Burnt toast, beef roast,
Old bones as hard as stones,
Big things, wig things,
Old things, gold things,
Fishes in dishes,
Crisp packets, tennis rackets,
That's what's in my bin!

Rory Findlay (8)
Widford School

Food Cupboard

White flour, lemon sour
Risk it, a crispy biscuit
Yummy sweets, ready to eat
Ground wheat, tidy and neat
Squashed tomatoes, sweet potatoes
Roast lamb, old ham
Tea and coffee, smells like toffee
Cheddar cheese, yes please
Old crab sticks, old dog licks
Jelly bowl, milk mould
And all very cold.

Elliot Calvert (8)
Widford School

The Magician's Cupboard

Hocus flowers, magic powers
Rusty hooks, spell books
Broken wands, mini ponds
Dusty elves on the shelves
Pointed hats, black cats
Stars and moons on balloons
Flying broomsticks in the air
Spreading dust everywhere
Dark and gloomy in this cupboard
So don't come in or you'll get flubbered!

Aidan Cooper (9)
Widford School

My Food Cupboard

A slimy cat
A packet of fat
A fishy fin
My joker's hat
A slimy fish
Some revolting chips
Chocolate shake
Micky make
All in my cupboard.

Kaitlyn Noy-Man (7)
Widford School

The Family Dinner

I was sitting in the car waiting, waiting
I was fidgety
And restless
And confused, waiting
I was jumpy, edgy and edgier
I was scared
So scared
I was uncomfortable, anxious
Who will I sit with?
What will the food taste like?
I haven't seen them for days, months, years, decades!
I'm eager
So eager
Who was it? Who? Who?
It was my family
Family for the
Christmas dinner.

Thomas Smith (9)
Wymondley JMI School

Swimming

I woke up, I was excited
I didn't know why,
At school I couldn't work,
At lunchtime I ate mine fast,
The teacher told me to slow down,
When I got back to class the teacher said,
'Swimming, let's go!'
When I got to the pool
I realised I forgot my trunks!

Samuel Blakey (10)
Wymondley JMI School

Run

I wait
I'm hot
The track is a long winding road
The golden sun is making me sweat
I'm scared
People are shouting 'Run!'
My legs are jumpy
I am determined
No, I'm not!
I feel like I'm falling off a cliff
I'm fidgety
My head is thumping *really* fast
Bang, bang, thud!
I'm hot
As I wait
I'm tapping my fingers
And then I *go!*

I am running
I feel sick
I have a headache
I fall
This is not happening
I hear cheers
People are saying my name
Have I won?
I have won!
That's brilliant!

Ashley Stead (10)
Wymondley JMI School

The Birthday Present

I looked out of the window,
Suddenly there it was:
Amazing!
Magnificent!
Astounding!
I was now as you might have guessed:
Excited,
Impatient,
(To get downstairs),
Nervous,
Worried,
(If something went wrong),
Nervously I start: biting my nails,
Fiddling with my hair,
Tapping the window sill,
I heard a shout, 'Come downstairs!'
I went downstairs: bouncing,
Hopping,
Skipping,
Finally I reach the door
And there it was, my first bike.

Emma Hayes (10)
Wymondley JMI School

Roller Coaster

The roller coaster judders as I travel up the track,
I'm panic-stricken, horrified.
Butterflies in my stomach are lashing to get out,
What if my alarmed tummy twisted and exploded!
My sweaty hands grip the bars,
A grim expression on my face, as I hang on for dear life,
Suddenly: a lash of excitement, we skid down the rail,
I'll never go on a roller coaster that judders on the track again!

Oliver Sunderland (10)
Wymondley JMI School

I'm Lost!

I looked around to
See if anyone was with me,
No.
Feeling uncomfortable,
I was left alone,
Wandering to the shops
To see if anyone was there,
No.
Wishing for people to turn up,
No.
Terrified, I staggered to the wall,
No one was playing in their garden,
My voice shouted, 'Hello!'
No one answered.
Trying to find my way home, can't.
It feels like I'm in a different world,
Where am I? I'm left alone.
I'm *lost!*

Charlotte Harwood (10)
Wymondley JMI School

A Roller Coaster Ride

I feel like I'm on a roller coaster of emotions . . .
Happy and fun then to miserable and sad.
I smile and I laugh but then I'm crying and uncomfortable,
The ride is slowing down and I feel much better than before,
Down and sad, to enjoying and exquisite,
This is so much weirder than ever before,
I'm amazed, I'm happy, my luck has changed
And my emotions have taken their course
And now I'm happy that it's stopped, stopped, stopped . . .

Reece Gould (10)
Wymondley JMI School

Waiting

Waiting on the sofa,
Worried, doorbell please,
Anxious, impatient me,
Drinking, sweaty me,
Jitters, unsettled me,
Tense, happen please,
Scared, what if: *no!*
Will I hear? Excited,
Then it happens:
I go out, others at home,
When we get back, *no!*
They were here, I wasn't! Unfair,
Having fun all of us digging in the sand,
Skipping, smiling, laughing, getting dirty,
My cousins and me, hope they stay,
Seems like only minutes they're here,
Seems like hours when I am alone,
Then they go, *no!*

Kate Adams (10)
Wymondley JMI School

Untitled

Hippo in the zoo
Lying in the mud,
When it hits the floor
It makes a big thud!

I'm the best roaring hippo
This world's ever seen,
Now I'm in the zoo
Setting this scene.

Jordan G L Allard (8)
Wymondley JMI School

Fly

It happened
So long before the day came
My whole life
Had become tense
Every day took years
But soon
The day I didn't want to come
Came
I sweated as I sat on the uneasy chair restlessly
I looked around me, lights were flashing
And my head was pounding,
I tore paper as
I waited, waited,
Waited for
The call
Of the
Pilot,
Fly.

Sam Tomlinson (11)
Wymondley JMI School

Swimming

I was at the pool edge,
My body was uncomfortable,
I was ready to dive,
The pool sparkled in the golden sun,
The small waves of the pool slowly came to the side,
I wasn't good at diving, probably the worst,
I dived,
The sensation was horrible,
It's like going into another zone,
I swam to the top,
Glad it was over,
Climbing out fast.

Jake Stead (10)
Wymondley JMI School

A New Life

I'm so excited about
having a brother or sister,
I am really nervous
but joyful.

I just can't wait
until its born,
there's going to be another
person in the world.

A new life,
I'm unsettled,
my heart's pounding,
I'm anxious, tense and fidgety.

I'm all sweaty,
I really want to know,
know if I have a
brother or sister.

It's here,
it's a girl,
it's a new life.

Demika-Leigh Owen (10)
Wymondley JMI School

Hope

Hope
All I could do was hope
Each thought in my head faster than the last
Like a tornado swirling round and round my head
I was uncomfortable, restless, I couldn't keep still
My heart was pounding hard against my chest
Level 3s or level 4s, what will I get?
I need to know now!
My body was tense, anxious, scared, nervous
Hope
All I could do was hope.

Sarah Fenton (10)
Wymondley JMI School

Haikus

On an autumn day
The colourful shining leaves
Flutter softly down

The leaves were pretty
In the misty windy air
Dancing busy leaves.

Thomas Burningham (7)
Wymondley JMI School

Walton-On-The-Naze

I had the jitters in my tummy,
I could not keep still,
All I could think about was that long blue strip,
I was longing for us to be there,
I waited impatiently.

The salty smell made me even more restless,
Then I saw it,
A long strip of silky material,
Chasing the sand,
I waited impatiently.

Getting off the coach was even worse,
I was so eager to get there,
From the word go I was off,
I sprinted down to the beach, but oh no . . .

My foot sunk deeper and deeper into the sand,
It was the fright of my life,
Alarmed and embarrassed,
I waited impatiently for someone to help.

The teacher helped me out of the quicksand,
Then back to the coach, still shaking from the shock,
I was a bit edgy about going back,
So I waited impatiently for the trip to end.

Lucy Keen (10)
Wymondley JMI School

The Queue

It was joyful in the queue,
Waiting for the terrifying moment,
But still waiting,
Excitement in the air,
But still waiting,
Closer and closer to the end,
Dreaming the magic second,
When you drop down
To Hell,
Then back up to Earth,
Everyone waiting
For the thrill
Of a lifetime,
Creeping forward,
Step by step,
But still you wait
And wait
And wait,
Suddenly silence
Falls on the crowd,
It was time
For the ride,
People were waiting for . . .
No longer waiting.

Jordan Price (10)
Wymondley JMI School

Haikus

On an autumn day
Flowers grow in rocky earth,
Leaves fall on the roofs.

Leaves blow in the breeze,
Golden leaves chasing around,
Scarlet, red and gold.

Laura Lambie (8)
Wymondley JMI School

A Poem To Be Spoken Silently

It was so quiet that I heard a giant bridge sway across the river.
It was so quiet that I heard the cloud and sky move at the same time.
It was so quiet that I heard a light flicker in the classroom.
It was so quiet that I heard a feather fall from a bird.
It was so quiet that I heard the world spin round.
It was so quiet that I heard a seagull squawking noisily.
It was so quiet that I heard a computer saying the word.
It was so quiet that I heard the volcano erupt far away in China.

Brett Ellis (8)
Wymondley JMI School

What Will It Be?

I feel:
Anxious, I tried so hard.
Nervous, not hard enough?
Hoping, I get a good mark,
Waiting, for the dreaded truth.

I know:
It's coming, there's nothing to stop it.
I'm uncomfortable and unsettled,
Impatient and scared,
But, maybe it will be inspiring.

A three?
A four
Or maybe even a five!
What will it be?

I can't take the waiting anymore,
I'm tearing the envelope,
Ripping it open,
I see the slip,
It drops . . .

Chloe Napier (11)
Wymondley JMI School

Swimming

I stepped onto the diving board,
Ready to dive into the warm, hot, refreshing water,
I was nervous almost scared,
Then I dived, I was whizzing through the air,
I did one, two flips then splash,
I hit the surface of the water, it felt warm,
Arms pulling, dragging, hauling me to the surface,
I popped straight out of the water
And climbed out of the pool, I did it again
And again
And again.

Liam Toomey (10)
Wymondley JMI School

The Earring

We're walking up the road, getting closer to the shop,
I'm anticipating having it done now.
What if it goes wrong?
Gets infected . . . gets stuck . . . starts bleeding . . .
But I have wanted it done since
I was little, a toddler,
But think of the pain,
I'm tense, anxious and
Excited, a funny
Combination,
I'm here . . .
It's done!
It wasn't so bad.

Charlotte Atkinson-Ryan (10)
Wymondley JMI School

SATs

Come out of school and I'm walking home, I'm so scared.
What will I get?
Will my parents be satisfied?
I'm nearly at the door now.
What will I get?
I open the door
And shout that I'm home,
My hands are all sweaty.
What will I get?
I sit down with my mum,
She has the envelope in her hands
And I'm hot.
What will I get?

Ryan Rushmer (11)
Wymondley JMI School

Tomorrow

I was petrified,
I knew that soon the day would come,
Tomorrow,
It would happen.
The time seemed to speed on.
Tomorrow.
It would come.
It would be like doom,
Tomorrow!

Edward Beard (10)
Wymondley JMI School

The Weird Birthday

It was my birthday
Yes, it was my birthday
With balloons and cake like a normal birthday,
A restless birthday,
An edgy birthday,
Waiting for guests,
A knock at the door,
In comes a monster and more,
It's a weird birthday,
A weird birthday,
An uncomfortable birthday,
A confused birthday,
An uneasy birthday,
A weird birthday,
A weird birthday.

Elliot Greenfield (10)
Wymondley JMI School

Autumn Haikus

In the autumn sun
Leaves fall down from air in peace
On a chilly day

When it was just dawn
All the leaves woke up and said
It's a new day now

When the chestnut tree
Gave all its conkers away
Children were happy.

Gemma Ward (8)
Wymondley JMI School

A Poem To Be Spoken Silently

It was so quiet that I heard the candle melting slowly on
the birthday cake.
It was so quiet that I heard the mouse squeaking in its mouse hole.
It was so quiet that I heard Elliot sit down on his bed.
It was so quiet that I heard the duck flapping its wings far away.
It was so quiet that I heard my heart beating inside me.
It was so quiet that I heard everyone breathing in the classroom.
It was so quiet that I heard my hair swishing from side to side
while I was running.
It was so quiet that I heard my friends whispering secrets.
It was so quiet that I heard the sunset change from red to
orange to pink.
It was so quiet that I heard a rabbit jump high up in the air.
It was so quiet that I heard my mum turn on the TV in the bedroom.
It was so quiet that I heard Mum peel the orange for her packed lunch.
It was so quiet that I heard a caterpillar turn into a butterfly.
It was so quiet that I heard myself blink.

Isobel Greenfield (8)
Wymondley JMI School

A Poem To Be Spoken Silently

It was so quiet that I heard a candle melting as it slowly burnt down.
It was so quiet that I heard the grass swaying from side to
side in the breeze.
It was so quiet that I heard an autumn leaf fall to the ground.
It was so quiet that I heard the clouds talk to me.
It was so quiet that I heard Lucy breathing in her sleep.
It was so quiet that I heard the wind blow.
It was so quiet that I heard Mr Carter open Tutankhamun's tomb.
It was so quiet that I heard my new tooth grow into my old gum.
It was so quiet that I heard the sun shine on the glittering grass.

Emilee Shaw (8)
Wymondley JMI School

A Poem To Be Spoken Silently

It was so quiet that I heard the salmon gliding in the golden water.
It was so quiet that I heard the clock going tick-tock on
the kitchen clock.
It was so quiet that I heard the breeze rustling the trees on the field.
It was so quiet that I heard the tooth fairy collecting my midget teeth.
It was so quiet that I heard Tutankhamun getting into his coffin.
It was so quiet that I heard a cheetah running a thousand
miles per hour.
It was so quiet that I heard a penguin swimming in the
South Pole seas.
It was so quiet that I heard a tree being cut down.
It was so quiet that I heard the wind rustling in the trees.
It was so quiet that I heard a raindrop running down the window.
It was so quiet that I heard a kookaburra pecking in Australia.

Alexander Garbas (8)
Wymondley JMI School

A Poem To Be Spoken Silently

It was so quiet that I heard a fly flying in mid-air.
It was so quiet that I heard a fragile flower move in the breeze.
It was so quiet that I heard Tutankhamun twitch in his dusty coffin.
It was so quiet that I heard an autumn leaf uncurling gradually.
It was so quiet that I heard a beetle scuttle through the
blades of grass.
It was so quiet that I heard a conker fall from the horse chestnut
tree and onto the long grass.

Roy Pugh (7)
Wymondley JMI School

A Rap Poem

Elephant in the zoo
Waving his trunk
He saw a mouse
And he wasn't a punk

Monkey in the zoo
Hanging on his tail
He started to scream
When he saw a snail.

Francesca B C Allard (9)
Wymondley JMI School

A Rap Poem

Elephant in the zoo
He was waving his trunk
Then he saw a mouse
And he wasn't a punk

Monkey in the zoo
He was jumping around
When he saw a snake
He screamed aloud.

Zoe Nichols (9)
Wymondley JMI School

Rap Poem

(Inspired by Jack Ousbey)

Fish in the river,
Waving its tail,
Put its head up
And started to wail.

It's the best rapping zoo there'll ever be,
It's tip-top, slip-slap, yip-yap for you to see.

Humza Chandna (7)
Wymondley JMI School

A Poem To Be Spoken Silently

It was so quiet that I heard a newborn chick flap its first wings as
it made its first flight.
It was so quiet that I heard a seed pop out of its smooth brown case.
It was so quiet that I heard the Earth shake as it spins
silently in space.
It was so quiet that I heard some mussel shells burst open
in a bubbling bowl.
It was so quiet that I heard Josie dream a surf dream in the night.
It was so quiet that I heard my hamster wake from his warm
day's sleep.
It was so quiet that I heard a satellite send a message to
a foreign country.
It was so quiet that I heard a caterpillar silently snoozing.

Sam Gilbert (9)
Wymondley JMI School

Autumn Haikus

In the shining sun
The leaves fall from the ash tree
Red and golden leaves

On an autumn day
Willow leaves fall to the ground
Floating, dancing leaves

Golden leaves fall down
On a shining autumn day
Crimson, scarlet, red.

Jade Taylor (9)
Wymondley JMI School

A Poem To Be Spoken Silently

It was so quiet that I heard Tutankhamun breathe from his tomb.
It was so quiet that I heard the candle melting on my birthday cake.
It was so quiet that I heard my heart beating softly while I was asleep.
It was so quiet that I heard the ground moving as I walked along.
It was so quiet that I heard the camels plodding through the desert.
It was so quiet that I heard my hair growing another centimetre.
It was so quiet that I heard the car from the city going along.
It was so quiet that I heard my new tooth grow through my gum.
It was so quiet that I heard a butterfly talking to the flowers.
It was so quiet that I heard a seed growing in the soft earth.

Kirby Halling (9)
Wymondley JMI School

Haikus

In the shining sun
Feathery leaves fall softly
To the soft wet grass

On an autumn day
Leaves dancing in the distance
Red and golden leaves

On a windy day
Willow swaying in the breeze
Leaves float from the trees.

Dekker Metcalfe (8)
Wymondley JMI School

A Poem To Be Spoken Silently

It was so quiet that I heard a tree growing under the ground.
It was so quiet that I heard the clouds moving in the sky.
It was so quiet that I heard the bits come off the rubber as
I rubbed out my drawing.
It was so quiet that I heard the feathers grow on a bird.
It was so quiet that I heard the water running through the drainpipe.
It was so quiet that I heard the school moving as I went in the door.
It was so quiet that I heard Tutankhamun arise.

Tom Marsh (8)
Wymondley JMI School

Rap Poem

(Inspired by Jack Ousbey)

Dicky bird in the zoo
Singing for me,
Mrs Farrel came along
And made it be
The best rapping zoo there'll ever be
Tip-top, yip-yap for you to see
Penguin in the zoo
Waddling in his cage
He's eight years old
That's his age
It's the best rapping zoo there'll ever be
Tip-top, yip-yap for you to see.

Heather Beard (8)
Wymondley JMI School